custom made

custom made

by Leslie Linsley

photographs by Jon Aron

Harper & Row, Publishers

New York, Hagerstown, San Francisco, London

FIRST EDITION

Designed by Jon Aron

Library of Congress Cataloging in Publication Data
    Linsley, Leslie.
      Custom made.

      Includes index.
      1. Handicraft.   I. Title.
TT157.L484   1979   745.5   78-69623
ISBN 0-06-012633-7
79 80 81 82 83 10 9 8 7 6 5 4 3 2 1

Contents

Introduction ix

Christmas Stocking 1

Holiday Gift Bag 4

Sewing Box 6

Candy Container 12

Appliqué T-Shirts 15

Hobo Storage Pockets 22

Doodle Art Greeting Card 24

Embroidered Child's Sheet 26

Beach Bag 29

Needlepoint Name Plaque 31

Friendship Frame 36

Graduation Memories 38

Busy Border Photo 41

Gingerbread Phantasmagoria 46

Stenciled Lunch Bags 53

Have a Heart Pockets 54

Scrimshaw Pendant 59

Recipe Box 63

Stenciled Sheet Set 66

Woven Name Banner 72

Stuffed Strawberry Pillows 75

Strawberry Sachets 77

Wood Type Assemblage 79

Embroidered Mittens 81

Fantasy Photo 82

Table Settings with Pzazz! 86

Party Tray 92

Alphabet Needlepoint 95

Grandmother Pillow 98

Valentine Surprise 100

Plexiglas Picture Frames 102

Photo Valentine 108

Ribbons, Rickrack, and Embroidered Trimmings 111

Personalized Appliquéd Emblem 112

Designer Stationery 115

People Pillows 122

Plant Holder 126

Party Apron 128

Heart Pot Holder 131

Needlepoint College Pillow 134

Formal Photographs 136

Batik Shirts 140

Xerox Transfer 146

Collector's Tote Bag 149

Monogrammed Clutch Purse 151

Designer Greeting Cards 153

Address Oval 154

Garden Basket 156

Embroidery Designs 158

It's the Process That Counts 160

Sources of Supplies 161

Index of Crafting Techniques 162

Acknowledgments

For me, writing a craft book is unlike writing almost any other kind of book. Before actually sitting at the typewriter, each project must be carefully determined, precisely executed, and directions worked out so that they are easy to follow. But most important, each project must be attractively designed. In order to include a wide variety of projects with equally diversified styles, many people have shared the crafting techniques that they have perfected. Jon and I want to thank them for contributing their time and work. Karen Kalkstein, Jane de Jonge, Rene Rudjinsky, Beverly, Rebecca, and Douglas Ellsley, Georgia and Dan McGurl, Ann Laredo, Don Hornung, Harriet and Ellen Doniger, Rose Jacobs, Louise Coe, Samantha Rochlin, Robert Quinn, Carol Arnold, Carol Davis, Ruth Linsley, Lisa, Amy, and Robin Brunhuber, Barbara Teiman, Pam Maglio, and Michael Aron.

Introduction

When I was little I used to enjoy shopping with my mother. She took my sister and me into many different kinds of stores and when she saw something she liked, she would say, "Let's not buy it. We'll make it ourselves." She didn't just say it. She actually made many of the decorative things that we uncovered in fancy shops. If it was something practical, she wouldn't hesitate to buy it, but when it came to those frivolous items sold only in gift boutiques, she felt it was wasteful to pay for what she knew she could make equally well. It wasn't only a matter of money. I think it had something to do with ego, a sense of confidence that she could make it better. And, inspired by what we saw, her creations *were* often better.

As I grew up I found myself reluctant to buy something that I felt I could or should make. Over the years I have taken the concept of making gifts for granted and have passed this tradition on to my children who can't imagine a home devoid of felt-tip pens, paint brushes, and at least twenty-seven different paint colors.

When I was a child, crafting was certainly not as popular as it is today, but it was easier to excel at it. Today there is so much more available and we are exposed not only to the different crafting techniques but to the very best teachers and experimenters. Craft shops, classes, books, and magazines are responsive to our desire for learning new skills in order to create beautifully handcrafted projects that represent our taste and talents. I think the crafting urge goes even further. A handmade object is a very concrete statement which testifies to the fact that we exist, something tangible that has been created from our selves. And when we make a craft gift, it is given and received with more feeling than one which has been purchased.

Craftworkers today have come a long way toward exposing their work. Craft shows, which were traditionally open-air, summertime affairs—more like bazaars than serious showplaces for professional crafters—are now year-round events almost everywhere in the United States. Many people have criticized the fact that crafts are not regarded as highly as art and therefore, in monetary terms, not as worthwhile. However, small boutiques as well as the large department stores are recognizing the value of carrying quality craftwork, affording the artists an opportunity to make a decent living through the sale of their crafts.

What does this do for the rest of us? As more of us try our own hands at crafting, we gain a sense of appreciation for work done by the very talented. The more we are exposed to creative techniques and good design, the more discriminating we become, and we are more selective when doing our own crafting. Therefore, when we give a handmade gift we want to be sure that it is at least as good as something which can be bought. Aside from this there is the opportunity to save money while creating something original that cannot be bought anywhere.

Somehow we feel less fearful about doing a craft project than attempting to paint a picture; perhaps because crafts began with the making of simple tools for everyday use and have traditionally been "of the folk." Also, many crafting techniques are quite familiar to us, such as sewing, stenciling, cutting and pasting—basic skills we all grew up with.

For years I have been designing craft projects. Some were conceived as gifts, but most were created to teach others new skills. The ones I have enjoyed making most were made especially for a particular person. There is an added enthusiasm which goes into the making of a personalized gift. The working in of a name, initial, or hobby of the receiver is a challenge, and certainly makes the gift that much more appreciated. I found it interesting that other craft-workers apparently feel the same way. Some of the people who have shared their work here have started small businesses selling their crafts. For this reason they have developed standard designs that can be repeated. However, it has been the occasional personalized design that got their creative juices going and made the crafting that much more enjoyable.

Almost any project can be personalized, either with the obvious—a name, an initial—or the more subtle use of a hobby, familiar quotation, memories of a vacation, a favorite song, poem, or a love of rainbows. Often something as frivolous as a favorite color, number, or bit of nostalgia is the perfect theme for a customized gift.

When I first started collecting ideas, I thought everything should be personalized with names or initials. But one idea led to another and soon I was saying, "Gary plays the harmonica, and what about Sharon's love for valentines? Everyone takes family snapshots. What we need are some clever framing ideas. Gardening is another favorite, and what about the Elton John lovers?" Birthday-month flowers, stationery, a college insignia, and hundreds of other ideas can be adapted for a custom-made gift.

I have very strong feelings about how a craft book should be presented. I try to adhere to these beliefs in order to achieve certain goals. First, the items should be worthy of the time and effort spent to make them. Next, something beyond the basic item should excite you. That something is a good design idea. It should be appealing in an interesting, out-of-the ordinary way. A well-designed project should be enjoyable to make. To me, this means not terribly difficult or involving impossible-to-understand techniques. If you can't figure out the steps involved, there is a feeling of frustration rather than a sense of accomplishment at having learned a new skill. If the techniques that are used are not too difficult, there is room for creative experimentation. The materials must be given careful consideration. They should be readily available and the cost should be commensurate with the time, effort, and end result. Recently, a popular magazine featured a personalized craft project. It was a casual table made from a 16-inch square wooden cube. The five exposed sides were covered with photo blowups of family snapshots. The instructions advised taking your photographs to a photo laboratory to be sized in order to fit the cube. I checked into the feasibility of doing this project and discovered that what had been described as "an inexpensive project" would cost a minimum of $350 to duplicate. This, in my opinion, was not a responsible presentation to the readers.

Another consideration is the instructions for making the projects. They should be complete and easily understood. Often, I am sure that I will be besieged with mail claiming that I must grossly underestimate the intelligence of my readers. However, often, when learning to make something for the first time, it is difficult to understand what might seem obvious to one who is familiar with the crafting technique. I for one cannot understand the most basic of knitting instructions and have absolutely no comprehension of the meaning of k1, p2. It might as well be another language. I am told, and it should be obvious from its popularity, that needlepoint can be done by anyone. Not true. Although Rose Jacobs, whom you'll meet later, has promised to make me an expert in one day!

So my goal is to present well-designed projects that are worthy of the time you will spend, to keep the costs to a minimum, to make the directions clear and complete, to expose you to some new crafting techniques, and to present design ideas that will show you how any gift idea is twice as nice when "custom made."

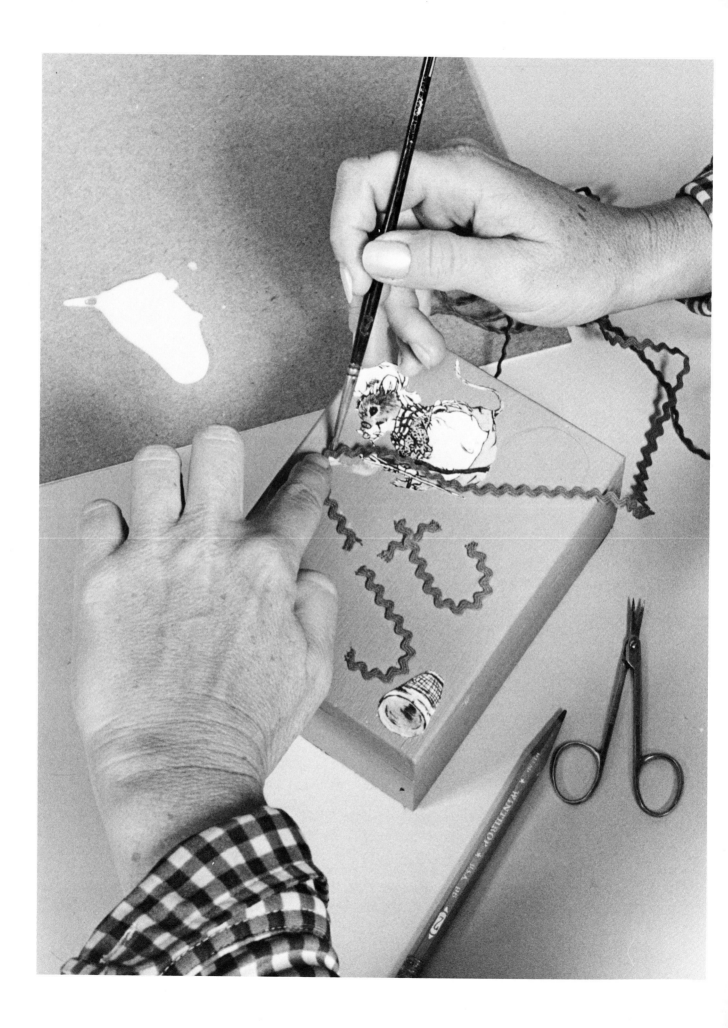

custom made

Christmas Stocking

Cut pattern pieces and rule diamonds in pencil.

Right after Thanksgiving I go into a holiday panic. Actually it manifests itself twice a year. Once in August when, in a fleeting desire to be superorganized, I decide to buy all my Christmas presents early. This mood vanishes when the sun comes out and the beach beckons, only to return to plague me at the proper time.

The special holiday issues of magazines do nothing to help put the whole affair in its proper perspective. I walk around with a big cloud of "should" over my head. I should make holiday cakes early. I should make new ornaments for the tree. I should finally design stockings for the girls before they are making them for their children. And what kind of Christmas memories will they have if I don't do my part?

Our Christmas stocking is easily made and is large enough for any goodies that Santa might leave. It employs the technique of quilt painting and is a lot of fun to make. You can also use this method for larger projects, such as a wall hanging. As for producing a real quilt in this fashion, the paint renders the fabric stiff and wouldn't work well for a comforter.

The materials needed are: a ½-yard of white cotton fabric, two or three tubes of acrylic paint in the colors of your choice, a stiff paint brush, scissors, pencil, ruler, stencil sheet, stipple brush, a ½-yard of cotton batting, a piece of felt or contrasting fabric for the back of the stocking, a ribbon for hanging.

Using the pattern scale stocking to indicated size, cut two pieces each for the stocking body, toe, and cuff. Trace ruled-off diamond

Apply acrylic paint to the fabric with stiff brush.

shapes onto the front body of the stocking. With right sides together match notches and stitch toe to stocking. Press seams open. Using a flat, stiff ½- or 1-inch brush, paint each diamond. If you use two colors—this one is red and yellow—paint all of one color before doing the other. Paint the heel and toe a third color. Let the paint dry thoroughly. The acrylic paint is permanent on fabric.

Cut a piece of cotton batting so that it is ¼-inch short of the edge of the stocking all around. Pin the back and front piece of the stocking together with the batting between. Stitch along the lines between the painted diamonds to create a quilted pattern.

With right sides together, join the cuff to the top of the stocking. Place right sides of the front and back stocking pieces together and stitch, leaving the top open. Clip around curved sections and turn the stocking right-side-out. Press under remaining edge of the cuff along the seam line. Fold the cuff wrong-sides-together.

Using small stencil letters, outline the child's name on a piece of scrap paper. Use this as a guide to center the name on the front of the cuff. Pick one of the stocking colors and stencil the name, using a very dry stipple brush and a small amount of paint. Hold the brush straight up and down and tap the paint onto the fabric until it's covered. For best results, use very little paint on your brush. Let each letter dry thoroughly before doing the next. If the paint is not dry before moving on, the letters will smudge.

Cut a piece of the cotton batting so that it is the same size as the front-cuff section. Slip this inside the folded cuff to pad it. Stitch around the outline of each letter to create a quilted name.

Slip stitch the top edge to the inside of the stocking. Fold out to form a finished cuff. Attach a satin ribbon at each side for hanging. I tied two bows at each side for an added touch. A wide lace trim can also be added under the cuff.

Each square equals 1 inch.

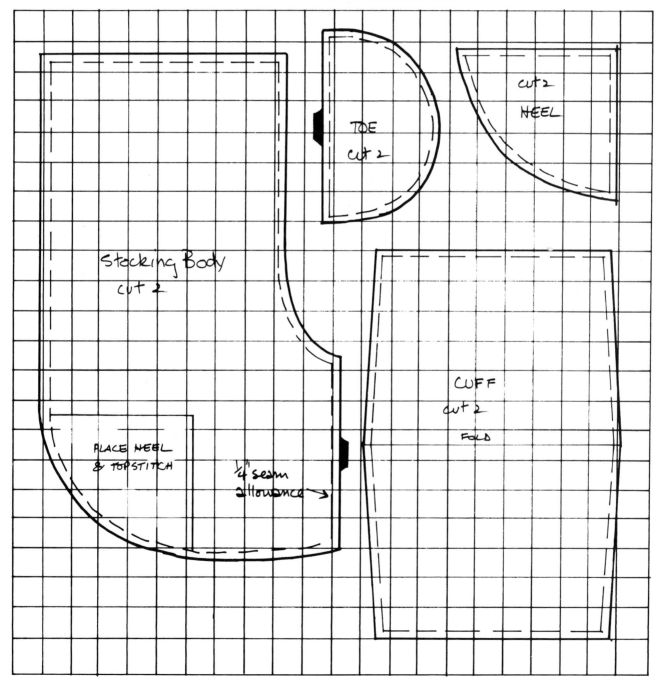

Holiday Gift Bag

If you would like to give a quick, inexpensive, last-minute gift that doesn't look last-minute, consider a bottle of wine in a holiday drawstring bag. Any fabric will do. I used bright green and white striped fabric, but you could use suede cloth or velvet for a more elegant bag or a calico print for a totally different look. Even a brightly colored or striped cloth dish towel might be unique. The only materials needed for this project are: fabric remnant; stencil sheet; white acrylic paint; stipple brush; yarn or ribbon for drawstrings.

Cut two pieces of fabric 7 x 15 inches. Hem the top edge of each piece by folding down approximately one inch. This is the hem for the drawstrings to run through. Before stitching up the bag,

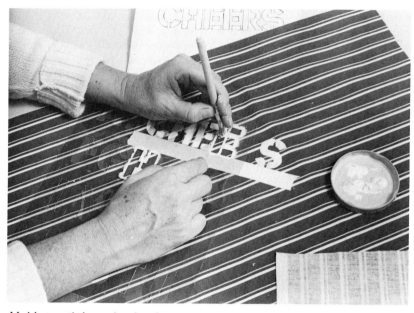

Hold stencil down firmly when painting.

decide on the placement of the word you want to use. It might say "Enjoy," or "Holiday Greetings," or even the name of the person. Using stencil letters that are available in a stationery or art supply store, outline your message on tracing paper. This will be your guide for placement of the letters on the fabric. If you place a piece of masking tape across the fabric it will be a guide so that the word will be straight.

Stencil each letter with white acrylic paint and a stipple brush. The acrylic paint comes in tubes and can be purchased in an art supply store. It has a water base and is very easy to work with. I have stenciled a lot of fabric, and after many errors, smudges, running, and much frustration, I can now pass on some tips. Use a clean stipple brush. Tape the stencil sheet to the fabric with masking tape. Hold the stencil down firmly on the fabric so that the paint doesn't get under where you don't want it. Most important, use a very dry brush with very little paint on it. Hold the brush straight up and down and keep tapping paint on the area until it is covered. Repeat the process as needed. Don't overload your brush; it is better to apply a little at a time for however long it takes to cover. The whole process takes more patience than time.

With right sides of the fabric together, stitch up three sides, leaving an opening at the top of one side just above the hem. I used red and green yarn for drawstrings and tied red Christmas berries to the ends. Colorful ribbons would be just as nice.

Sewing Box

A small sewing box is a good gift because everyone likes to have mending materials handy. If you do a lot of sewing, chances are you have your materials well organized or contained in a sewing basket. But when you just want to replace a button or take up a hem it is convenient to have the basic needle and thread, small scissors, and occasionally even a safety pin in a small handy holder. This also makes a great going-to-college gift, because it is useful but often forgotten. Personalize it with an initial or name and stock it with everything for instant repair—a few buttons, straight pins, safety pins, needles, small scissors, and two spools of black and white thread. Guaranteed to be appreciated.

This box is decoupaged using a paper greeting card and rickrack trim for the design. If you know what the recipient's favorite color is you can use it for the background.

Materials needed are: rectangular wooden box, rickrack trim, acrylic paint, brush, a small piece of fine sandpaper, paper design, scissors, Elmer's glue, varnish, paper for lining, small piece of heavy fabric (such as corduroy or felt), a small piece of cotton batting.

Decoupage is the eighteenth-century art of applying cutout paper designs to a surface, preferably wood. Originating in France, it was primarily applied to furniture. As decoupage is most commonly done, many coats of varnish are brushed over the cutouts so that they are completely coated, thus creating a smooth surface. Today the craft is rarely practiced on such ambitious pieces, giving way to small boxes and plaques, which have become very popular with those who do decoupage. Therefore, small wooden boxes are easily found in craft shops and come in a variety of sizes. Stocked primarily for decoupage, they are usually made of smooth and light basswood. Some are hinged, others have a removable top. I recommend the hinged boxes whenever you can find them.

Begin by sanding all exposed surfaces of the wood until it is smooth. Next paint the outside of the box as well as the inside rim. Acrylic paint gives very good coverage and is easy to apply. The color range is fantastic. However, if you already have regular indoor or latex wall paint use it. I always keep a quart of white latex paint to mix with acrylic for the color of my choice. Often the acrylic paint colors are too intense to be used straight from the tube.

A ½- or 1-inch inexpensive sponge brush is perfect for this project. Rinse it in water between coats. You will need two coats of paint to sufficiently cover the box. When it is dry, sand lightly with a fine grit sandpaper such as 3M WetorDry #200 or #400.

Select your design from a greeting card, wrapping paper, or book. Magazine paper is too thin and will wrinkle and tear when

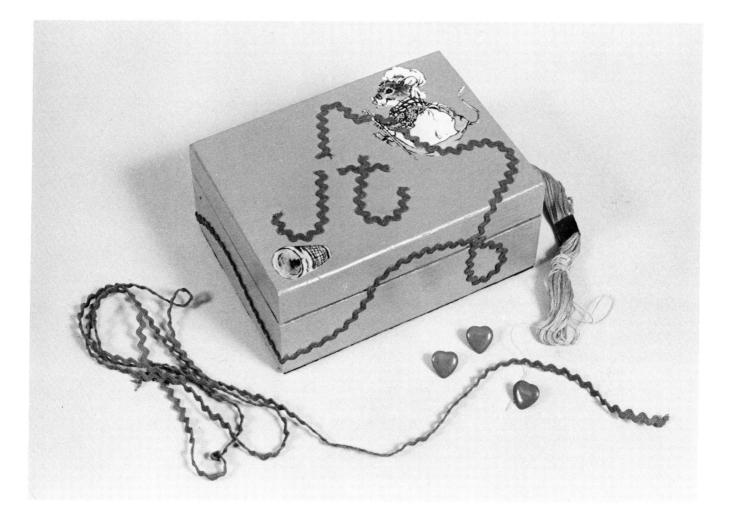

applied. Also, when varnishing, the print will show through from the other side. Other design selections could be a photograph, wedding or birth announcement, or pressed flowers. Select a design that relates to sewing or to the person. It might simply be a pretty picture that fits the box. You might want to create a scene using several different design elements. I wanted to relate my design to sewing and spent a lot of time in the card shops before finding one that I could use. Cut the design apart and add to it as you like. This mouse was doing some embroidery with a huge needle. I cut her out, leaving what I didn't want to use.

For the best cutting results use a curved-blade cuticle scissors. Straight scissors leave choppy edges and it is not as easy to go around curves and hard to get at areas. All excess paper should be cut away. Yes, even between stems and leaves and other tiny sec-

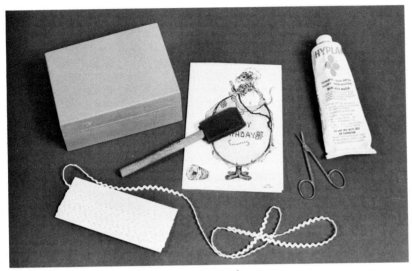

Material needed for a decoupage sewing box.

tions. If you leave any white paper, unless you have a painted white background it will show up and ruin the look of your design.

Place your cutouts in position on the box and move them around until they create a pleasing arrangement. I used the rickrack trim as though she is sewing with it. First spread Elmer's glue (any white glue is fine) on the back of each paper cutout and, with the palm of your hand, press firmly on the box. Wipe away any excess glue with a damp sponge. Next draw a pencil line where you want to place the rickrack. The initials are created so that it looks as though they have just been sewn on. Using a pointed paint brush, toothpick, or your finger, apply the glue along the pencil line. Starting at one end, lay the rickrack along the glued line. Press down as you proceed. Keep your hands clean so that the rickrack won't stick to you and lift up. Extend the design down onto the front and sides of the box for interest.

The lining for this project is wrapping paper with a small red-and-white print. It seems to go with the rickrack. A pin cushion is created for the inside of the lid. Measure and cut the pieces for each side and bottom of the box. Cut four strips for the walls of the top. Do not line the inside lid. An extra piece can be cut for the bottom or you may prefer a piece of felt. Spread each piece with glue and press into place. Trim any excess paper with a razor blade.

Protect the box inside and out with a coat of varnish. Do not varnish the inside of the lid where it has not been covered with paper. Semigloss, indoor wood varnish is used to create a hard,

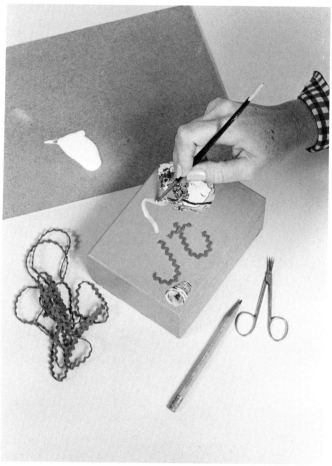

Apply a line of glue with a paint brush.

Place rickrack down onto glue.

smooth finish. This takes a full day to dry. If you are in a hurry to finish this project, you can use fast-drying polymer medium found in craft and art supply stores. It will not create as smooth or hard a finish, but will protect sufficiently. It is necessary to apply three to five coats of varnish or polymer medium. Each must dry thoroughly before reapplying. The polymer medium has a water base, so the brush used for painting can be used again. A natural hair-flat varnish brush is best for the varnish, which has an oil base. The brush must be cleaned in mineral spirits between applications. An alternative for this is spray varnish. Krylon spray varnish is excellent because it can be applied quickly, easily, and dries within twenty minutes. I always introduce the long-drying wood varnish, however, because it creates the best decoupage finish you can get, but the choice is yours. Spray is fine for this project.

9

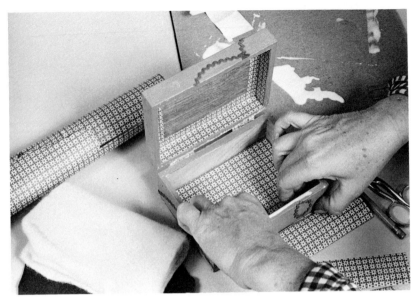

Cut pieces of wallpaper or wrapping paper for lining.

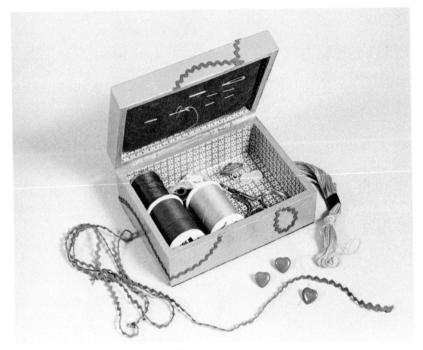

Pin cushion is glued inside lid.

Measure the inside of the top and cut a piece of fabric so that it is slightly larger all around. Clip the corners off. Lay several layers of cotton batting on the fabric to form a puffy cushion. Apply plenty of glue to the inside top of the box. Turn the edges of the fabric in over the batting and set this in place on the glue. Clean your hands and press the pin cushion down firmly until it is secure. Press around on the edges. A butter knife can be handy for this.

For a final touch, lightly sand all exposed wood areas except the rickrack. Rub on a coat of clear paste wax, such as Butcher's, for added luster.

When giving this gift you might wrap it in the lining paper and tie with matching rickrack. This sewing box was made for Janice Turner, who enjoys sewing and is a college student. Appropriately, like a famous singer, her nickname is JT.

Candy Container

Decorative glass and plastic jars make especially nice gift containers for a variety of candies. Fill one with jelly beans or bubble gum to give to a child. Wrapped, hard candies in different colored paper look pretty in the jar also.

Robin and Carla are in high school and, like many teen-agers, constantly try to stay on a diet. Realizing that all dieters like to occasionally cheat, Robin gave Carla a jar of her favorite candies. Just in case there was any question about it, she personalized the jar with a reminder, "Carla's Diet Busters."

Ordinarily it is difficult to stencil or paint on a rounded or curved object, especially one that is glass or plastic. However, with the aid of clear, plastic Contact, anything can look as though it has been printed. The Contact is available wherever household items are sold and is bought by the yard. A half-yard is more than enough for this project, and you can use it to print on other things as well.

Materials needed are: a jar in desired size, clear Contact, scissors, ruler, acrylic paint, stipple brush; sheet of stencil letters.

Decide what message you would like to stencil on your jar. You may prefer to simply apply a name or initials so that the jar can be used for anything once it is empty. Using a scrap piece of paper, outline your words in pencil. This will be your guide for placement. You can check to see if the words will fit around the jar and adjust accordingly.

Draw a line across the Contact or use masking tape as a guide so that your stenciled letters will be straight. Robin used red paint because it is bright and shows up well, but choose the color you like best. Almost any color will be bold enough on a clear background. Acrylic paint is recommended for stenciling. It dries fast and is the right consistency for good coverage. Squirt a small amount in a shallow dish; a plastic coffee can lid is perfect. The stipple brush, available in art supply stores, should be held straight up and down. Tap the brush on the paint so that there is very little on it. Do not overload the brush with paint as this will cause smudging and possible running under the designated area to be filled in. Tap up and down in quick movements on the stencil letters. Each letter should dry before proceeding on to the next. Cut the stenciled strip of Contact.

The Contact has a paper backing that is peeled away in order to expose the sticky side. Peel away approximately 1 inch of paper from the edge where your words begin. Place this securely in position on the jar. With one hand peel the backing off while smoothing down the Contact with the other. If this doesn't go on smoothly, lift carefully and redo. Be sure that no air bubbles are trapped underneath. Wrap the Contact around the jar, pulling it tightly as you do this. Once secure, the paint and plastic wrap are fairly permanent

13

Wrap the strip of Contact around the jar.

and the jar can be washed when needed. I don't think it will hold up too well in the dishwasher, however.

Fill it, wrap it with bright tissue paper, tie with a ribbon, and perhaps a candy or two tied in the bow. For a variation, if you are really sworn off candy, try a jar filled with potpourri. Either make your own, using dried rose petals, or buy a sweet-smelling mixture in an herb store.

If you would like to make a potpourri it is easy enough if the flowers are in season. In my book *Wildcrafts,* I experimented with many varieties and discovered that the roses were the easiest to dry and the scent will last almost forever. Simply let the roses dry in the sun with plenty of air circulation. The dried petals can then be put in a glass container. Keep this away from the light so that the color doesn't fade. Once dried, the jar should be kept airtight to keep moisture out. If you would like a mixture of scents and color, lavender leaves and blossoms have a beautiful fragrance. Combine these with the rose petals and you might add the leaves of lemon verbena, geraniums, sage, and woodruff. For another kind of potpourri try dried citrus peel. Toss all the dried leaves and buds in a bowl. To this add a fixative such as Orris root, available from a florist, nursery, or where herbs are sold. Add a teaspoon of spices and if you'd like, a drop of fragrant oil or your favorite perfume. Toss the mixture in the container. From time to time, if you have more dried scents, toss them in, too. Stir the mixture up occasionally. And there you have it, a nondiet buster.

14

Appliqué T-Shirts

Appliqué is decorating with small pieces of cutout fabric that are stitched to a larger background, usually fabric. Like decoupage, which is applying design using cutout pieces of paper, appliqué comes from the French and means to lay on. There are two kinds of appliqué. One is for the more uninhibited, letting one's imagination run wild, creating a free-form design with fabric pieces sewn to a background. The other is for those who want to know beforehand how the finished project will turn out. This appliqué work is based on careful planning of a design. A rough layout is first drawn on paper to see how it looks, then it is worked precisely as planned. Either way, the results are a creative expression of the designer.

While appliqué is an art form, enabling us to make such things as exciting wall hangings, it is also a decorative craft. Many craftworkers use this technique to adorn a variety of existing items. Clothing, pillows, and bedspreads are only a few of the things that can be personalized with the addition of creative appliqué. Working with simple, graphic, solid shapes, even the beginner can enjoy the excitement of turning a pile of scrap fabric into an interesting design.

Carol Davis and JoAnn Carbonier are two creative women with good business sense. They were seeking a vehicle for their combined talents. It was after taking a contemporary patchwork course that Carol became interested in appliqué. The teacher, a well-known craftworker, placed a great deal of emphasis on color as well as technique. "I've always had a good feeling for design and she opened my world up that much more," Carol says. That course, more than anything else, was the beginning of a design and business career for Carol, who teamed up with her friend JoAnn Carbonier. They began collecting remnants of fabric and playing around with ideas. The variety of patchwork and appliqué pillows in Carol's beautifully decorated home attest to this.

JoAnn is a former teacher. Remembering the large letters used in the classroom to teach children to spell, she redesigned these for a new venture. With a wealth of design and color ideas, Carol Davis and JoAnn Carbonier began to appliqué T-shirts. "At first we didn't think this would become a business," she smiles. Now, boxes overflow with orders to be delivered, drawers bulge with calico, striped, polka-dotted, colorful fabrics. Another contains a variety of threads as well as scissors and other sewing aids. The well-equipped sewing machine is very prominent. "We started by taking our shirts to a local boutique. From there we were approached by a mail-order house." Carol opened the catalog to a beautiful full-color photograph featuring two models wearing T-shirts from Patchworks, Carol and JoAnn's business. Their most popular designs are red strawberries on a white shirt or the word LOVE appliquéd on a tennis shirt. To keep up with their orders, the women spend their time creating new designs, hiring other women to execute the sewing once everything is pinned in place. In this way, Carol and JoAnn can work from their homes, control their hours, and make it possible for other women to earn money at home as well. Since they both have families, this arrangement is ideal.

Carol agreed to share their alphabet designs as well as giving directions for making an appliquéd T-shirt. Best of all, for me, was her choice to use my name for the design. "I really shouldn't attempt to do the final sewing since JoAnn does it much better," she protested. But since JoAnn was busy for the day, Carol completed the project, which I am proud to wear.

Begin with a shirt that you will enjoy working on. Many T-shirts are made of thin cotton and after several washings become limp and out of shape. The T-shirts from Patchworks are made of soft, weighty cotton and are the more expensive ones found in better clothing stores. This type of shirt will make the finished project look all the better. If you want to make an appliqué of a simple design, you can find pictures to copy from coloring books and similar sources where the objects are bold and well defined. Use the letters provided for name appliqués. Scale them to the size that will be appropriate for your shirt.

Unless you are a fabric collector, which even many nonsewers are, spend some time in a fabric shop. Select a variety of fabrics with small prints. Each letter is too small to show much of a large print. Since you will need only a small amount of each design, try to buy remnants. It is good to have a combination of different colors and patterns to choose from. Carol suggests gingham, checks, polka dots, florals, thin stripes, geometrics—in light and dark colors. All of the appliqués are first bonded. This is important to give lightweight fabric body. Easy Shaper is a brand name and is best for this project. It is fused to the fabric by ironing it onto the back before each letter is cut out. When the women buy a bulk of fabrics they iron the bonding material to the back before storing it. When they are designing, this saves a lot of time since the fabric is ready to use. Carol stresses the aspect of color, not just pattern combinations. The thread color is another way in which you can achieve a contrast. It doesn't have to blend with the dominant color of the name. If, for instance, the design is mostly red and yellow, you could use blue thread. The thread is both a necessity for attaching the appliqué as well as a decorative consideration. While the shirts from Patchworks are stitched on a zigzag machine, you can do this work by hand, creating a similar decorative stitch.

16

Sample shirt shows a variety of names.

Trace template on back of fabric, backwards.

One of the best things about appliqué is the materials needed. There are few and they are basic enough so that you might be able to start without having to make any purchases. You will need: a good, sharp pair of scissors, pencil, ruler, scraps of fabric, a piece of tracing paper, pins, needle and thread or sewing machine, T-shirt, iron, cutting board (optional), and Easy Shaper bonding material.

Begin by scaling up the letters that will be used. Carol used all lowercase letters which measure 2¾ inches high. If you have a longer name, each letter must be smaller, or about 1⅞ inches.

Trace the letters that you have scaled. Next select the fabric to be used for each letter. Try to create a pleasing balance with color and design so that each letter looks well by itself and as part of the overall design. You might begin with a color scheme and try alternating dots, checks, and floral prints, for example. Place a piece of the Easy Shaper on the back of each small section of fabric to be used and iron it down.

You can either transfer your traced letters to heavier paper, then cut out each letter to be used as a template, or transfer the traced letters directly onto the back of the bonded fabric. Either way, when doing this, be sure to place it backwards. In this way it will read correctly when turned over to the right side. Cut out each letter using very sharp scissors.

Try the arrangement of letters on your work table to see how they relate to one another. If something isn't quite right, make a new letter in another fabric. It doesn't take very long and is better than making do. Carol works on a fold-up cardboard Dritz cutting board when pinning the letters. If you don't have this, she suggests the carpet rather than a hard surface.

Smooth the shirt out so that it lies flat. Lay the ruler across the front, lined up with the underarms. Center the word right and left. Carol and JoAnn prefer a layout of letters that slightly overlap each other so they appear scrunched together. You may want to leave spaces between your letters. Either way, be sure they are absolutely straight.

Stick a straight pin into the top and bottom of each letter to hold it in position. This is the reason for working on a cardboard or carpeted surface. The pin is up and down, not in and out. Remove the ruler, reach under each letter and pin in place. Be sure that the letters don't shift as you do this. It is important to take care to pin accurately. If the letters overlap you don't have to be concerned with the spacing. If not, each letter should be the same distance apart. It might be wise, at this point, to baste the letters just to be sure.

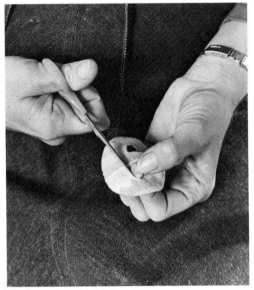

Cut out bonded fabric letter.

If you are using a sewing machine with a zigzag attachment it will be set at approximately 3½ width and done with a slightly open satin stitch. Carol suggests playing with the tension, as each machine is different. Practice on a piece of scrap fabric first. Remember that you are sewing to stretchy fabric. Therefore you should maneuver the material carefully when shifting it. Sew from right to left, underlining the entire word. In other words, rather than stitching each letter (when using Carol's close layout) you will treat the word as a solid design and go around the outside before stitching details of each letter. Carol used a blue denim thread for my shirt, figuring I'd wear it with jeans. Have a variety of threads on hand to choose from. When finished sewing, go over the project and cut off any loose or scraggly end threads. For a final step, press the shirt with a steam iron.

Carol Davis and JoAnn Carbonier's business is successful and they are enjoying what they're doing. However, Carol says that she is thinking about starting some more exciting projects, like wall hangings. With a flair for decorating, she'd like to be doing more in this area. Now that you know how to create an appliqué you might think of other applications as well.

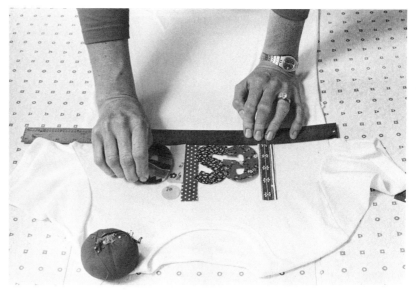

Pin letters in place before sewing.

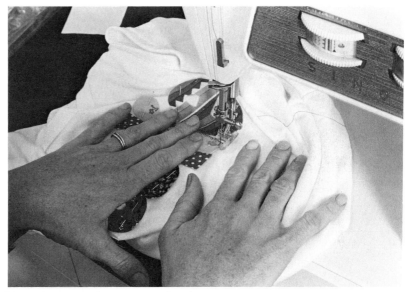

Use a zigzag stitch to sew appliqué.

Appliqué designs by Carol Davis and JoAnn Carbonier.

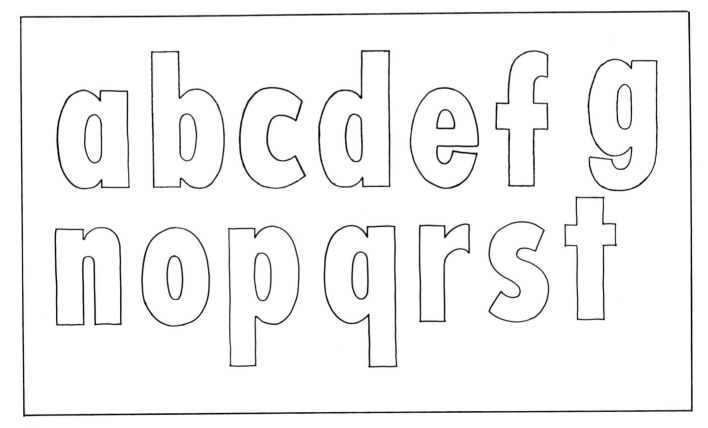

Hobo Storage Pockets

What happens to the one sock that mysteriously disappears in the laundry? I suppose the odd assortment of clothing that our children lose is residing somewhere. However, that odd sock always turns up right after I've given up looking and thrown the lone match away. Then there is the pair of worn-out jeans that become cutoffs that never get too worn out to wear, only too small. The gym shorts from last year and the T-shirt that shrunk, a mitten that another child left behind are all potentially useful recycling items, believe it or not. These castoffs can be incorporated into an overall wall unit of storage pockets.

Could anything be more personalized? The jeans that she wore sailing over the Fourth of July weekend, shorts from a winning basketball game, one of the gloves that were worn during a ski weekend when she brought home the new friend's cap—all nostalgic reminders of when and where the clothes were worn.

Select a solid fabric for the background. The material should be heavy enough to hold the weight of objects that will be contained in the pockets. The background should also be large enough for the layout that you plan, using the clothes on hand. This will take some rearranging beforehand. I started with a pile of odds and ends and spread them out on the floor, adding and eliminating until I had the right combination.

The material used here is heavy cotton and the finished size, once hemmed at top and bottom, measures 40 inches by 40 inches.

The materials needed for storage pockets.

The blue plastic grommets are sold in a package at some hardware and Army and Navy stores. The package gives easy-to-follow directions which, basically, tell you how to hammer the two parts together. A large mallet is perfect for this. The grommets will keep the fabric from tearing at the holes and will finish it off.

Lay each object on the background and handstitch around the outline of each. You might want to add some trim to dress up the overall look. I added ribbon-and-lace trim to Amy's jeans and stitched her name on the back pocket. The Nantucket button was hers, as was the flower pin, which I added to the hat. You could add some embroidery or other imaginative decoration.

For hanging use inexpensive plastic self-adhesive hooks that are found in hardware stores. These hooks are barely perceptible and are extremely effective. Measure across and level the hooks so that they correspond to the grommet holes. Hang the pocket unit and fill with appropriate objects. A storage unit like this could be most helpful in a small child's room, where toys seem to find their way onto the floor rather than out of the way. This could also be used in a hallway to organize hats and mittens when not in use.

Doodle Art Greeting Card

Lisa Brunhuber is a college student taking a design course. She has developed a style for creating her own greeting cards that her friends look forward to receiving. Lisa calls her alphabet "puff letters," because they look like soft clouds. We've reproduced the alphabet here so that you can use the letters as initials or names for many projects.

Lisa adds her own whimsical drawings of animals, spiders, an owl in a tree, a ladder leading to a rainbow, an upside-down umbrella catching raindrops, and Oreo cookies inside round letters. Having always worked with children, Lisa has a feeling for what delights little kids and often her designs reflect a bit of fantasy. The objects she draws are always combined into the overall work so that they create a scene.

When making your own cards, add as much as you want, incorporating shapes that might relate to the person who will receive the card. Colored pencils or good felt-tip pens, such as Magic Markers, are used for coloring the designs. The letters are usually outlined but not filled with color. This, of course, is a personal choice.

Regular drawing paper is used to make a card. Art stores have different-sized pads as well as blank envelopes in varying sizes and colors. It might be wise to find the envelope before making the card so that you don't end up with a huge card and no envelope to fit.

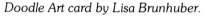

Doodle Art card by Lisa Brunhuber.

Embroidered Child's Sheet

Lisa's puff letters were an inspiration for the embroidery on a child's sheet. This can be a delightful gift for a new baby. The small crib- or carriage-size sheets lend themselves to this project, or, you might prefer to apply the design to the hem of a pillowcase.

Embroidery is like painting with thread. It defines shapes and fills in outlines with color. Embroidery was the medium that supplied the decorative element lacking in textiles, and with materials from local manufacturers, early American needlewomen worked very intricate patterns. Much of it was influenced by their earlier English counterparts. Like other crafts, embroidery had its origin in the daily needs of humanity. Joining two seams together was a problem that could be solved decoratively, and the natural instincts to indulge in decoration, rather than mere utility, must have been felt.

Today we have a bountiful source of designs and supplies to draw upon. There is no question that needlework has become a more popular, creative pastime than anyone could have predicted. Craft shops, department stores, and mail-order houses have responded to the increasing demands for materials. Using color alone as an example, there is virtually no color that cannot be found in embroidery thread that you might need for a particular piece. The stitches are so basic that even the novice can complete a project with almost no instruction.

The materials needed are: black cotton embroidery thread, a variety of different, bright-colored threads, needle, scissors, embroidery hoop.

To begin this project draw the letters that you need for your name. Each one should connect with the one before and after it. Choose the designs that you like, or that correspond to our project and draw them in place here and there over your letters. Color in the design in order to see which colors will look best. This will help you to visualize the final design, and you can take this to the store when selecting your embroidery thread.

Rub pencil over the back of the design and place the tracing over the section of the sheet that will be decorated. In this case I found the center of the top hem of the sheet. Remember that the sheet will be folded down, so be sure to plan this for the right side. Tape the tracing to the sheet and go over the outline with a ball-point pen. The design will be transferred onto the sheet in faint pencil markings.

An embroidery hoop is important for insuring smooth work. It will hold the section of the fabric you are working on very taut. Bright colors will look best for this project since it will be used for a

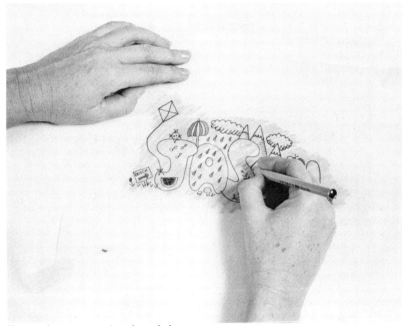

Trace design onto border of sheet.

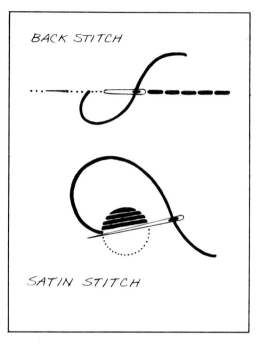

child. The designs are small and may require separating the threads so that you are working with only two strands. Use an embroidery needle with an *eye* large enough for the thread to pass through easily without breaking. A thimble can save you a lot of pain. Have a pair of small, comfortable scissors handy to cut the thread after each object or color. Most of the stitches used for this are straight or satin stitches with a few improvised versions in tiny areas. Work with one hand on top of the fabric and one below. Your work will go faster, you will feel more comfortable, and the thread will be more uniform. When doing embroidery for any length of time you begin to feel the tension and, while this may sound terribly elementary, sit in a comfortable chair with good lighting on your work.

Begin by outlining the word with black thread. Keep the stitches small and close together. This is done with a running and backstitch. Work a backstitch by bringing the thread through on the stitch line. Next work a small backward stitch through the fabric. Continue to outline each letter by bringing the thread through again, a little in front of the first stitch. Take your needle back again by pushing it in at the point it just came through. From there you will fill in all the other areas of the design, adding accents and shading where called for. When finished, press the embroidered area from the back using a steam iron.

Beach Bag

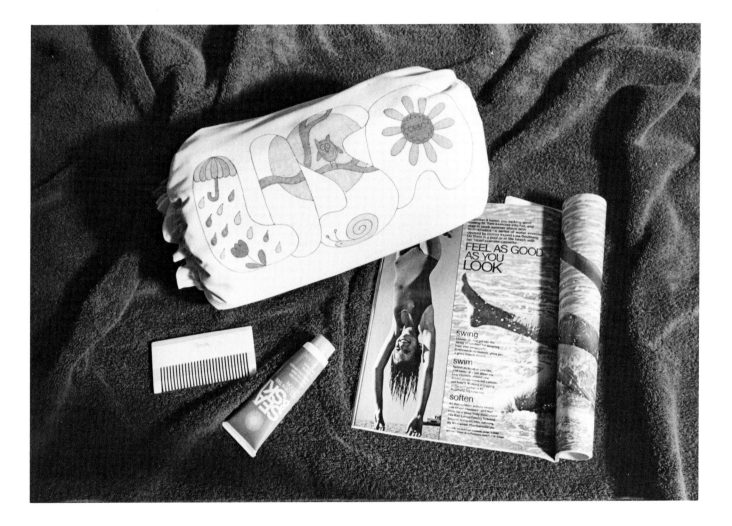

This bag is decorated with Lisa's puff letters and whimsical designs. It can be used as a beach bag or as a tote to hold toiletries. The lining is made of plastic material and can be found in hardware stores, if not the fabric shop.

Materials needed are: ½-yard of white broadcloth cotton, canvas or duck; fabric markers in a variety of colors (available in craft or art stores); scissors; ruler; ½-yard of clear, plastic material; 44 inches of cording or cotton braid; straight pin.

Draw the letters of your name on a piece of paper. The size that you use to scale the letters will depend on the length of your name. Next draw the designs you've selected to include around the letters.

Make a pattern to size from tracing paper. Place the larger piece so that one long side is on the fold of the fabric. Cut two pieces.

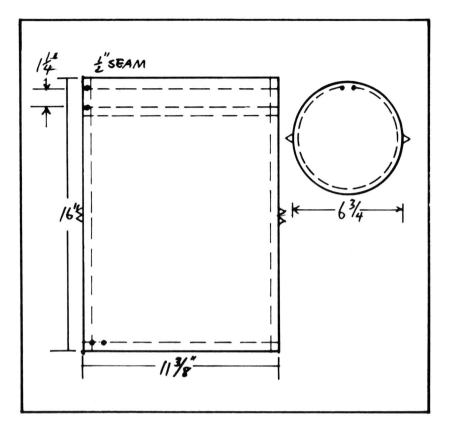

Cut one round piece for the bottom. Cut these same pieces from the plastic as well.

Determine where on the fabric you will put the design. It should not be too close to the seam line. Using your paper layout as a guide, transfer the design to the fabric. Outline all letters with black fabric marker. A regular marker will bleed on the fabric. Color in the design with the fabric markers. An alternative to the colored design could be embroidery. Also, fabric pastels are fun to use. They are available in art supply stores. First you color the design right on the paper. This is done on the underside so that the design reads backwards. Center the paper, right side up on the fabric. The crayon or pastel coloring will be against the material. With a hot iron transfer the design to the bag.

To make the bag once the design has been applied, stitch double-notched edges of the sides together, leaving an opening between the dots on the pattern. With right sides together, pin the bottom to the lower edge of the side, matching small dots. Stitch and trim the seam.

Next, stitch double-notched edges of the plastic lining together. With right sides together, pin the bottom lining section to the lower edge of the side lining, matching small dots. Stitch and trim the seam. Turn the lining right side out and slip inside the fabric bag. Turn both top edges inside and stitch along the top edge of the bag. To form the casing for the cord, stitch along stitching lines at each dot. Insert the cord through the casing channel and tie the ends into a knot.

This finished bag is large enough to hold a beach towel as well as other small items. You might like to add a pocket to the outside for sunglasses.

Lisa Brunhuber coloring design on fabric.

30

Needlepoint Name Plaque

Rose Jacobs and Harriet Doniger have been advising women on needlepoint since before it became a craze. Twelve years ago Rose had a needlecraft shop and "Things haven't changed all that much over the years," she says, referring to buying trends. Now Rose and her husband own the Hartsdale Home Center in a suburb of New York City. Teaming up with her daughter Harriet, the two women totally renovated what was once the basement area of the store. Today it is a bright, colorful, expansive room, boasting everything that the needlepoint enthusiast, whether a beginner or lifelong craftsperson, could possibly need. Cubby areas hold the variety of beautifully dyed wools; finished work in sophisticated, cute, exciting, unusual, and recognizable designs fill the walls; a long table invites the craftworker to sit down for help; another table is set up with all the designing and painting materials, and along another wall, a vast array of already painted canvases are displayed for the choosing.

Rose and Harriet design their own canvases and keep hundreds of ideas on file at all times. They are good at what they do, primarily because they are tuned in to their market. They know trends, and their loyal customers know that Rose or Harriet can accommodate their needs. Best of all they are enthusiastic. After many years in the business, Rose's personality still bubbles with excitement over each new design. And she is equally encouraging when customers return again and again for help during the execution of their work. Classes go on intermittently, but Harriet keeps her design materials in constant use. "I am always thinking of a new idea," she says. "And

Carefully outline design with black marker.

when you're surrounded all day by your work, you keep growing and getting better."

While we were chatting, a woman came in with a Vasarely needlepoint that she had just finished. "That's marvelous," Rose exclaimed at seeing her own rendition carried out in stitches. The original hung on the wall, one Rose had executed herself.

Since I wanted to stick to projects that are personalized, Harriet agreed that a name plaque was probably a good project to demonstrate. Her daughter Ellen, an equally experienced needleworker, was enjoying a school holiday and decided to help her mom. Perhaps this project is one that your son or daughter might enjoy working on. I was told that young people learn to do needlepoint much faster than adults.

Begin by tracing the letters provided here, in order to create your name. Scale this to the desired size. Be especially careful to make the space between each letter the same. Next draw a rectangle around the name, leaving 3 inches on each side and 2 inches at the top and bottom. This will become your frame size.

Select designs from elsewhere in the book and draw them around the letters where they look best. You might want to create your own characters. Outline the entire design with black Magic Marker so that it is bold enough to see under the mesh. Place a piece of tracing paper, or better, visualizer paper (available in art stores) over the design. From this you will make a color sketch. Fill

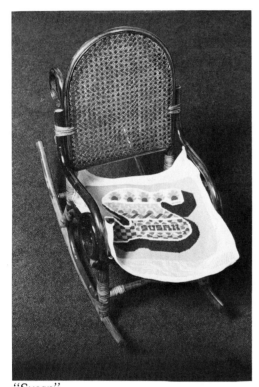

"Susan"
needlepoint for pillow by Rose Jacobs.

Harriet works with daughter Ellen Doniger.

in colors with a variety of markers, watercolors, or colored pencils. This should be a lot of fun and the most enjoyable part of creating a design. Do a few sketches until the colors work well together. If uncertain, look at the color plate of the "Jennifer" plaque. Your sketch will serve as a color guide for buying yarn and will help when doing the needlepoint. Harriet suggests a strand and a half to do a square inch.

Tape the artwork to a tabletop and place the canvas on top of it. Be sure to lay the canvas over the sketch so that it is correctly in position, leaving the 2 inches all around for blocking. Carefully trace the black outline of the entire design onto the canvas with Magic Marker. This will take patience to do neatly. Harriet is particularly good at this and has perfected her technique through experience.

What you now have is your original design transferred to canvas. This will help to key your yarn colors. Harriet always fills in the designs with the exact color, at the same time making a key on the side of the canvas. You can fill in the designs with Magic Marker if this will make your work easier. However, with your color guide, you really shouldn't have to do this.

The project can be done using a flat stitch throughout. When selecting a frame, choose a color that will match a color in the pattern or one from the room where it will hang. Rose reminds her customers that wool needs air to breathe; therefore, your piece can be blocked and framed, but should not be put under glass.

33

A B C D E F G

H I J K L M N

O P Q R S T U

V W X Y Z ! ?

Enlarge to desired size.

If you don't want to bother making your own design you can send your name to the Home Center where they will paint the canvas and select the yarn so that it will be ready for you to stitch. In that way you can simply do the needlepoint. The canvases that Harriet designs are all sewn and finished off on the edges with twill tape. (For information see the source list.)

Some of the expert needlecrafters, who have been helped by Rose and Harriet, have worked on projects that are good examples of some ideas that might inspire you. The large "M" initial worked by Pam Maglio is used as a seat covering. It is a blend of dusty rose with darker shades of pink. The green, leafy vine adds a delicate touch, softening the initial design. The background is creamy white.

A director's chair is a big undertaking, but adds whimsy to a child's room. As a focal point it is certainly worth the effort. Harriet's son Billy is a soccer player, so it seemed appropriate for him to have a sports chair designed by his mother. Another version of this was designed by Harriet and worked by Barbara Teiman for her daughter Rachel. The theme is Noah's ark.

Rose Jacobs and Harriet Doniger are always willing to help anyone with his or her needlepoint problems. If you cannot find the supplies you need, Rose will be more than happy to mail them to you. The little rocking chair is an item that they import. When accompanied by a small initialed needlepoint pillow, this makes a darling gift for any child. This too can be ordered from her by mail.

34

"Noah's Ark" design by H. Doniger.
Needlepoint by Barbara Teiman.

Sports chair by Harriet Doniger.

Bench cover by H. Doniger. Needlepoint by Pam Maglio.

Friendship Frame

Amy and Liz are friends and the photograph of them suggested doing something more than simply framing. The idea for this is just an example of the hundreds of ways that you might take advantage of photostating something that has meaning to you. Anything that is printed can be made to the exact size needed for your project. For this background the definition of the word "friend" was taken right from the dictionary and increased in size to fit an 8 x 10-inch frame.

A photostat is different from a photocopy because you can reduce or increase the size of the original that you are copying from and it will be absolutely black and white, rather than gray. Photostat services are listed in the yellow pages of your local telephone directory and many copy centers provide this service. A photostat is referred to as a "stat."

This project was planned for an 8 x 10-inch frame, but you can use any size and the directions will be exactly the same. They sound more complicated than the process really is so don't let it throw you. This is a very simple project to do. You will begin by drawing a rectangle the size of your frame, in this case 8 x 10 inches, on a

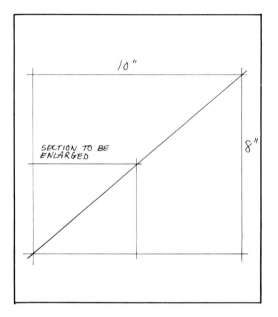

Materials needed to have a photostat made.

piece of tracing paper. This will serve as your positioning guide and is very important to do accurately. Draw a diagonal line through the rectangle. Lay this tracing over the section of the dictionary to be enlarged.

With the dictionary words lined up in the lower corner of the larger rectangle draw a smaller rectangle around this definition. The width of the column of type will determine the width of the smaller rectangle. The height is then determined by the point at which the two lines of the small rectangle come together on the diagonal line (see drawing).

Take the tracing paper layout with the dictionary to the photostat center and give them the whole thing with instructions to make a negative photostat. It may require two steps to get the right size, but the stat house will know what to do. This will cost approximately four dollars.

The photograph you use with this background should be fairly small in order to dramatize the effect and to have a contrast between the background and photo. The photograph you choose might have a white border which should be trimmed. Use a metal ruler and razor blade to get this exact. An 8 x 10-inch plastic box frame was used to give the project a contemporary feeling. When creating your own, keep in mind that frames come in standard sizes, so don't use an odd dimension.

Graduation Memories

This is a project that requires precision. This is not a problem for most people. Others are apprehensive about doing such a project. As a craftsperson of long standing, I have become comfortable with the knowledge that craftwork can absorb quite a bit of human error. For this reason, perhaps, I have gravitated toward crafting. If I had my way I'd probably spend all my time designing projects, then wave my magic wand, at which point an army of little elves would appear to transform my designs into finished projects. This is not to say that I don't enjoy almost all craftwork, but there are times when I'd like to see the results before putting in the time.

When I met my love, my life changed in more ways than one. I shared my living space, my dreams, my aspirations, and my assumption that nobody is perfect. I have often described crafts as having a charmingly crude quality; the human element being accounted for and praised. Jon is a graphic designer. He didn't buy it. His world is filled with measurements that are perfect. Not approximate . . . exact. Inevitably some of his ways have filtered into my work and I can at least admit to the merit of doing some projects with more care than others. And yes, even taking the time to use a T-square, straightedge, and razor rather than eyeballing a project and lopping off the excess paper with a pair of scissors and a shrug. And I must also tell you that it has been fun, although I will still defend my position when pressured.

In the past I wouldn't have considered doing a project like this, thus I would have been limiting myself and depriving you of a few really good ideas. Therefore, in all honesty, I must credit Jon with this one, which for him is child's play.

The objective is to combine a photograph with a graduation diploma, making one composite framed picture. This may look like a photograph pasted in the center of a diploma, but it's not quite that simple. There is no need to cut up, alter, or use your original diploma other than for copying. Further, most diplomas are not the exact size needed for a background to fit any snapshot. Also, you might want to eliminate some of the writing in order to dramatize the effect. Once again we used the photostat process described in the Friendship Frame project. The photograph is a 5 x 7-inch color print. The frame is 9 x 12 inches.

The materials needed are: a graduation diploma (or similar document), a 5 x 7-inch snapshot, black construction paper, tracing paper, rubber cement, black marker, metal ruler, X-acto knife or razor blade, one push pin, 9 x 12-inch frame.

Begin by making a 9 x 12-inch rectangle on a piece of tracing paper. Draw another rectangle 5 x 7 inches in the center of this.

This will be your layout guide and is important. You will use this to position your diploma, photograph, and type correctly. When we placed the tracing over the diploma there was just enough room for the school name and seal above the photograph and the word "diploma" and the date below the photo. Roughly pencil in the words on the tracing paper so that you will have a complete guide to show you how the finished project will look.

In order to eliminate the extraneous type from the diploma you will have a photostat made. In this way, of course, you can keep your original diploma intact. The original is used to copy, not destroy.

Look for a photostat service center in the Yellow Pages under Photo Printers or Photo Copies. Take your diploma to them and ask for a negative photostat to be made from your diploma. Take the negative photostat, which is made of paper, and cut away the portions that you want eliminated. Tape the 9 x 12-inch tracing guide to a piece of black construction paper. Your goal is to position the pieces cut from the photostat in relation to the photograph. The

Diploma and negative photostat.

Pasteup and final stat.

lines of type over and under the photo should be centered and parallel to one another.

Before mounting the type in position, blacken the edges of the photostat paper with black marker. Apply rubber cement, available in art stores, to the back of the type and place these strips in position on the construction paper. Do not mount the photograph at this time.

Take this paste-up to the printer and ask for a positive. It should be made larger than 9 x 12 inches so that it fills the frame. Place your tracing paper guide over the positive so that the type is in position. Trim the white border off the photograph and spread the back with rubber cement. Lift the tracing and mount the photo in place.

Mark the four corners of the 9 x 12-inch rectangle with a push pin. With a metal straightedge and razor or X-acto knife cut out the rectangle between the pin points. This must be accurate. It is now ready to frame.

If you want to give a gift to parents or grandparents of the graduate it is just as easy to have two photostats made at once and the cost will be approximately two dollars apiece. Can you think of a less expensive gift that is so great looking?

Busy Border Photo

For years my daughters have brought home their school photographs. Some have been framed; others, that they were more critical of, went into the photo album. This project was inspired by these pictures that seem to be well suited for a whimsical background. You can use the artwork that we created or design your own with the borders provided.

This project was designed to fit in a 9 x 12-inch standard picture frame. If you use the art provided this couldn't be simpler to create. Take the page of this book to a copy center where they make photostats (described in the previous projects) and tell them to

Making the border.

make a negative photostat increased 162 percent. This will reverse the black and white as you now see it on the page. If you want it to be exactly as shown you will have to have a negative made first as described, then made as a positive photostat. The person at the stat house will be able to help you. The cost will be approximately four dollars.

Trim the photostat to 9 x 12 inches and carefully cut out the center hole with an X-acto knife. Tape the photograph with adhesive tape behind the opening and set the whole thing in a black frame.

If you want to create your own background, follow the step-by-step directions that we used to make this one, using your own selection of borders provided here. If you don't want to cut up the page, take the book to have the page photostated for about two dollars.

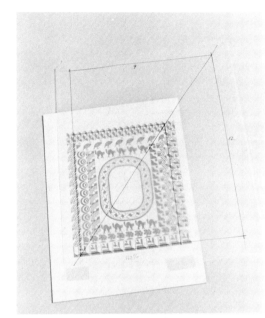

Enlarging art for 9 x 12-inch frame.

Photo, original art, and negative photostat.

You will need a T-square and triangle to do this project accurately. Make concentric borders using a different border on each side. The photostat is heavy paper and can be cut up easily. Paste each border down on an illustration board with rubber cement. (Both are available in art supply stores.)

Take this to the photostat center and tell them to make a photostat enlarging the art to 9 x 12 inches, or to your frame size. Trim this paper, if necessary, to fit your frame. Carefully cut out the center, tape the photograph from behind, and set into your frame.

You can have a lot of fun with a project like this. Almost anything can be photostated, and you might find something in a book that you want to use without having to first cut it up and rearrange it. Take the design of your choice to the copy center and tell them the size that you want. It can be enlarged or reduced to fit your needs. Before doing this project check the Friendship Frame and Graduation Memories projects for complete details about finding a photostat copier and other tips.

If you have a black-and-white background and would like to color it, use Magic Markers or watercolor dyes, such as Dr. Martin's or Pelikan, available from art supply stores.

43

44

45

Gingerbread Phantasmagoria

Nobody celebrates Christmas quite like Beverly Ellsley. She is the closest person I know to being Ms. Claus. Even with a hectic work schedule she finds the time to welcome the season in full-blown MGM style.

Beverly is a talented much-sought-after interior designer. She also builds homes, is capable of completely redoing any house, is an expert on restoration, and specializes in creating authentic country kitchens. Her designer rooms have appeared in the decorating magazines regularly and what is remarkable about Beverly is that she is self-taught. The project that Bev and her children shared with us was created in an environment no less enchanting than that found in a fairy tale.

Bev lives with her husband, Bob, and their two children, Douglas and Rebecca, in an exquisite log cabin house. It was a snowy afternoon. A fire crackled in the enormous old-fashioned fireplace. Lace and patchwork stockings hung from the mantel. Large rolls of satin ribbon and lace lay in wait on the stenciled living room floor (another of Bev's talents). Some of the twenty-foot-high windows had already been framed with trimmings. One wall of glass windows offered a view of the vast expanse of snow-covered trees and chunks of ice that were caught on rocks at the winding river's edge.

Inside, the Christmas tree, an extravaganza that magazines vie for the privilege to photograph, is Bev's crowning achievement. She says, "I think we bought this house because of the high ceilings. As soon as I walked in I saw my Christmas tree blinking in all its splendor, reaching to the top of the room. That was it. This room was built for a fabulous Christmas tree." Beverly has definite Christmas traditions which she hopes Douglas and Rebecca will grow up with and pass on to their children. One of her traditions is making gingerbread houses. Each child designs his or her own house, which is duplicated according to their own drawings. Every year their fantasy houses change. This year, for instance, Doug wanted a log cabin house like the one they now live in. Becky always wants a house loaded with dripping frosting and lots of candy charm. A real Hansel and Gretel house. "Becky always puts as much on her house as it will possibly hold," Bev explains. "And she does it quickly. No fuss or bother or planning. She just goes at it . . . usually ending up with as much on her as the house. It reflects her personality. Total abandonment. Doug on the other hand is more meticulous. He takes his time and makes it neat. He's very definite about what he wants and plans more carefully." Bev takes the children's drawings and uses them to make a pattern to cut the house sections from the sheets of gingerbread. "I think we've gotten a little out of

Gingerbread house by Rebecca Ellsley.

Douglas Ellsley testing to see if icing is ready.

hand this year. Every year they seem to make the houses bigger and bigger," she says, adjusting the roof on Doug's house. This is more personal and certainly more fun than the traditional pre-planned gingerbread houses that come in a kit. Bev says that the pieces can't possibly be perfectly matched working this way, but the crudeness is extremely charming. Also, a great deal of measuring and planning is eliminated, leaving time for much fun and decorating. "The important thing," Bev says, "is that the kids feel like it's their creation. It is their very own house that they'd like to live in." They begin the houses a week or so before Christmas and leave them on display until the day after Christmas when they are gobbled up, well, not all in one day.

Bev suggests cutting out the pieces and baking the gingerbread the day before. Children want to get on with it and don't have a long attention span. They will be impatient waiting for the cooling and assembling of the house before starting the decorations if it is all done in one day. Make extra pieces for accidental breaking.

Jon and I were waiting for Bev and the children to have a free day to decorate their houses. Bev had already made the gingerbread and the basic house shells were constructed. We arrived. The camera equipment was all set up. Becky, Bev, and I filled bowls with candy kisses, red-hot hearts, gumdrops, shredded coconut (for

Bev adjusting new roof on Doug's house.

snow), candy canes, peppermint circles, sour balls, colored chocolate balls, and miniature Santas. The icing was beginning to harden
in the mixing bowl. Suddenly Bev waved her arm, knocking Doug's
house over and creating a near disaster.

It was early evening. The candy began to disappear as the new
house finally emerged. Becky, totally oblivious to all that was happening, just kept covering her house until it was brimming. Spurts
of giggles contrasted with Doug's frustration over having to wait as
Becky expressed her glee each time she added more to her already
elaborate creation. We had forgotten to restrain her, which, it
turned out, made for more fun.

Before you begin making a gingerbread house with your children, find a large, heavy piece of cardboard on which to place the
house. It should be large enough to add a front path and decorations around the yard, if desired. In this way the finished project can
be moved out of the kitchen.

You will need about six boxes of Betty Crocker gingerbread mix
for each house. Roll the gingerbread out on a large cookie tin. Cut
out the child's paper drawing to use as a pattern. Use a knife to cut
out each piece of gingerbread. You will need two identical pieces
for the front and back and two for the sides. You will also need two
pieces for the roof. Measure these carefully so they are large
enough. Cut four pieces for a chimney, if desired, and one for the
front door. Cut away a triangle shape in the middle of two chimney
pieces if they are to fit over the peak of the roof. You might want to
make lines crisscrossing the roof pieces to simulate roof tiles. Cut
out sections where windows are indicated. Little extra details can be
made as well; a tiny doorknob, window boxes, a porch—all made
from the gingerbread. However, the simpler the design the easier it
will be to put together. Bake the gingerbread according to the package directions.

Place a medium-sized pan on the low burner of your stove and
pour about two cups of sugar into the pan. This will begin to boil.
Keep stirring so that it doesn't burn. It will begin to look like molas-

ses. This will be used to glue the sections of the house together. The mixture gets very hot and will cause a bad burn if it gets on your skin. Keep the children away from the stove while doing this.

When building the house, you should work quickly before the sugar cools. Hold the back section of the house in one hand and one side in the other. Dip the edges that will be joined into the hot sugar so that these two edges are completely coated. Hold these together while placing them upright on the cardboard. Take the front and opposite side pieces and join them in the same way. In order to join these two "L" shapes, dip a knife into the hot sugar and spread it over the edges. Stick the house together and hold for a second or two while cooling. Spread the sugar on all exposed edges and attach the roof pieces carefully. Do not press down too hard. Something may crumble.

Join the four sides of the chimney in the same way. Then spread the sugar over the bottom edge of the chimney and attach this to the roof peak where it will look best. As you can see, Douglas's house is not very conventional and, in this case, calls for a bit of improvising. You may find that pieces don't join absolutely perfectly

since they have changed shape slightly when cooking. However, fill in where necessary with more sugar glop and keep in mind that anything can be covered up with frosting and decorations. Now the house is ready to be turned over to its creator.

The icing is made from confectioner's sugar, water, and egg white. Beat this up until it is stiff. We didn't start with any precise measure, just kept adding sugar and water until the frosting was a good consistency for spreading without running. This year Bev bought a complete set of cake-decorating accessories and recommends a frosting tube for the job. The frosting is squirted along all seams and around windows and the doorway for a ruffled effect. This will cover up the dark sugar lines where pieces connect. When we weren't paying attention, Becky used the knife to spread frosting all over, but Bev says it looks better if only the roof is covered.

Next comes the real fun. For Jon and me it was most enjoyable tasting the different candy until Becky caught us, "Hey, you're eating up all my decorations!" Have a good variety of different colors, shapes, and sizes on hand. If you empty the packages into different bowls it will make the selection easier when deciding where

to place them. Besides the candy, Rebecca thinks tiny marshmallows make the best bushes around the house and for lining a path. Gumdrops can be useful for this. Sprinkle coconut over the roof and around the cardboard.

While this project is a messy one, everything washes off clothes, hands, and floors, and the joy is worth the effort. This is a project that should be given plenty of time, and then some. As it turned out, when we got through, nobody could think about dinner. We'd already dined on frosting and candy kisses.

Doug was still carefully designing his new house when Becky announced, "I'm through. Gotta go." We carried the house into the living room and placed it under the tree laden with unusual handcrafted ornaments. "Quick, quick, take my picture with my very own house," Rebecca said impatiently on the verge of taking off.

Stenciled Lunch Bags

Stencil names with colored markers.

An inexpensive but delightfully personalized gift for a child is his or her own lunch bags. Many kids don't bother with lunch boxes because they have to carry them around all day. A brown-bag lunch is often more convenient . . . for big kids, too!

With a felt-tip pen, crayon, or paint and a plastic stencil sheet you can have a lot of fun. One snowbound afternoon I really went wild stenciling every child's name I could think of. Big letters, lowercase letters, initials, numbers, even names spelled backwards. I tried different colors and materials.

A package of one hundred sandwich bags is as close as your nearest grocery store. The stencil sheet is a standard stationery store item. If you want bright, sharp letters that look as though they are silk-screened or printed, use acrylic paint and a stipple brush. But for a quick, television-watching-time project, a colored marker is easier.

Draw a pencil line as a guide and start stenciling. If you're doing the same thing over and over it gets boring, so change along the way. Do initials over the entire bag or whatever your imagination dictates.

When finished, tie the stack with a bright ribbon and stick a candy stick or lollipop under the bow.

Have a Heart Pockets

A graphic fabric design can be an inspiration for a project. The design of white hearts on a bright red background is especially attractive and lends itself to a variety of projects. I am crazy about hearts. I have a friend who will buy anything with hearts or rainbows on it. Perhaps you know somebody who has a favorite something. This is a good way to use it. There is almost no color, pattern, or subject that can't be found in fabric. The storage, heart-shaped pockets are practical for holding small, lightweight objects within easy reach. Hung in a young girl's room, it is a handy wall unit next to the bed. If placed against a white wall, you might repeat this fabric or a busy overall heart pattern for curtains. The fabric used for this can be ordered from Fabrications in New York City. They also have an outlet in Boston, but I spoke to the people in the New York store who said they could fulfill a mail order. (See source list for information.)

Materials needed are: a ½ yard of 44 to 45-inch-wide fabric, ½ yard of white cotton broadcloth, scissors, pencil, needle and thread, small tube of red acrylic paint, stipple brush, sheet of stencil letters, 36-inch wooden dowel.

The runner measures 16 inches wide and 41 inches long, therefore a ½ yard of fabric will leave you plenty of extra for hemming. Fold each side under, press, fold again, press, and stitch to finish off the side edges. Turn the fabric under, making a 2-inch hem at the top and bottom to hold the dowels.

Cut hearts from fabric.

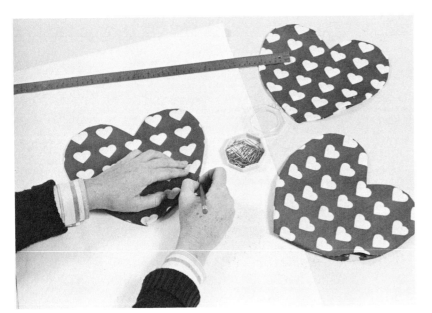

Make a faint pencil mark for heart placement.

Use tracing paper guide for stenciling.

Create a heart by tracing our half-heart pattern twice. The heart can be used same size. Plan how best to cut six heart shapes from your fabric. Each heart pocket need be finished and lined only on the top where it isn't attached to the runner. However, for extra weight, I recommend doubling the whole thing. With right sides together, stitch around the edge, leaving a 2-inch opening. Trim excess and clip on curved areas. Turn inside out and press.

Measure down 6½ inches from the top of the runner and center the heart so there are approximately 3½ inches between each side and the outer edge. Make a tiny pencil mark on either side of the heart as a guide. Do this with the other pockets. There are approximately 4½ inches between each pocket. Pin the hearts in place, making sure they line up between the pencil marks. Carefully hand-sew these to the runner, leaving the top curves of each heart open. The heart fabric creates a self guideline, as my stitches stop at the top completed row of hearts.

Tap brush up and down to cover stencil area.

Choose the words that best fit the objects to be held in the pockets. I used French words for fun. The plastic sheets of stencil letters are better than the ones cut from paper. These are available in stationery as well as art supply stores. Make a guideline by tracing the letters on paper, lining them up and spacing evenly. Place a piece of masking tape across the fabric where you will stencil a letter. This will aid in assuring a straight line. Stenciling on fabric can be tricky. A few tips will enable you to do a clean, neat job. Use a medium-sized stipple brush. If you use a paint brush, it should be one with stiff, square bristles. Tape the edges of the stencil sheet onto the fabric with masking tape. Work from a shallow dish of paint. The acrylic paint, in this case Grumbacher red, should be fairly dry. If it is too wet the color will bleed on the fabric. Keep the brush dry and work with very little paint at one time. Holding the brush straight up and down, tap repeatedly over the letter to be stenciled. Do this carefully so that no paint seeps under the stencil. Always work from the edges inward. When the area is covered sufficiently, lift the sheet.

Let the paint dry on one letter before going on to the next. With so much dark stenciling on a white background there are bound to be a few smudged areas. These can easily be corrected with a spot of white paint. With a fine, pointed brush, touch up messy areas where needed. Don't worry, the touch-up will blend right into the background.

Cut a 36-inch-round wooden dowel in half. Paint the ends that will show. You can use the acrylic paint, or if you have red spray paint, use it. Insert the dowels through the top and bottom hems of the runner and hang. I used self-sticking plastic hooks that you can barely see.

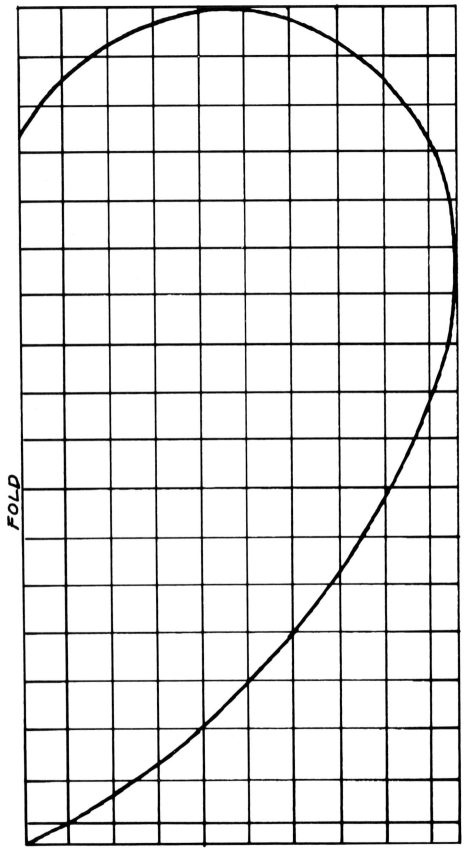

FOLD

Use pattern same size.

Scrimshaw Pendant

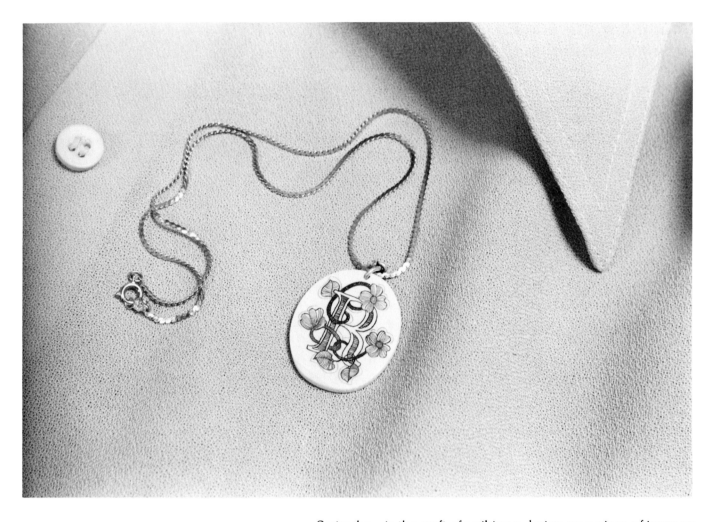

Scrimshaw is the craft of scribing a design on a piece of ivory or bone in order to produce decorative objects, jewelry, and useful items. It is one of our first American folk crafts, having originated during our nation's earliest years among New England whalers. While on the long whaling voyages that lasted sometimes for two or three years, the sailors would relieve the boredom by drawing and scribing on whale's teeth and bone.

Much of our history is depicted in the drawings found on whales' teeth, exhibited in maritime museums. Contemporary craftworkers have been influenced by the work of their forebears, but have added new dimensions to the craft for today's appeal. If you have a facility for drawing, you will be able to design and scribe an original design; if not, you can trace any design or use one of our initials. Obviously, it is not so easy today to find a whale's tooth to work on. However, many craft shops do sell ivory discs and they can also be ordered by mail. (Check the supply list in the back of the book.) For a substitute material you might use plastic. Scrimshaw can also be done on the inside of an ordinary seashell, such as a clam or scallop. A regular beef bone can be boiled and sanded until smooth then cut with a hacksaw in order to create napkin rings or a key ring. The bone, when cleaned, is as smooth and white as ivory and takes the scrimshaw process quite well. The rest of the materials are readily available in art stores and they are few and inexpensive.

Materials needed are: object to be scrimshawed, scribing tool, such as an X-acto knife or old dental tool, pencil, black India ink, a variety of colored inks or watercolor dyes or oil paints, fine, pointed artist's brush, small piece of sandpaper (fine grit), rag, piece of wire or jewelry finding, and a chain or ribbon for hanging.

Begin by sanding the material you are working on until it is smooth. A shell makes a good practice piece for developing your technique and is so smooth that sanding isn't required. Next, trace the design you have chosen. If you look through books you might find a small design that is just right for your object. If you apply one of the initials supplied here, the design will fit onto a small 1½-inch disc. Transfer the tracing onto the disc by rubbing your pencil over the back of the paper. Lay this onto the disc and retrace the design. The pencil marking on the disc will be faint, but visible enough to follow. Each penciled line will be scribed with your sharp tool.

Press the scriber down and scratch into the surface. You will begin by outlining the design. A magnifying glass might be helpful for this. With a pointed artist's brush go around the scribed outline with India ink. Next, wipe away the excess ink, leaving only that which has penetrated into the scribed outline. Now you will determine where you would like to add color. For each color there is a new set of lines. If, for instance, you would like a flower to be purple, you will incise thin lines close together on each petal. Carefully paint the petals with the purple dye. Wipe it off before it can dry. The color will remain in the scribed lines, but will come right off the clean surface. If the color dries, simply wet the rag slightly and rub the excess away. The dye will settle in the scribed lines, creating a purple flower. With a bit of practice you will be able to do very intricate work, adding interesting details. Each time you want to add more detail it will require more scribed lines, each filled with more dye or ink or paint, whatever you are using. The oil paint can simply be rubbed on with your finger. For brighter colors the dyes are preferred over the oil paint. The dye can be purchased in small bottles. (The most common brands are Dr. Martin's or Peli-

Carol Arnold making scrimshaw necklace.

Materials needed for scrimshaw.

ABCDEF GHIJK

LMNOPQRSTUV

WXYZ&

1234567890

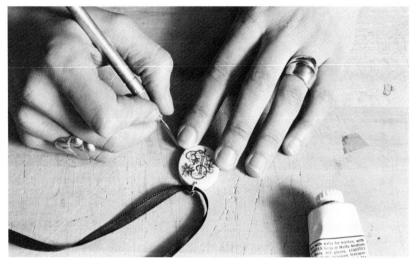

Trace and transfer initial to be scribed.

kan.) If one color runs into another while adding detail, it is quite simple to redye the first section to bring out the color again.

A small hole can be drilled into the top of the disc in order to insert a small loop for the chain or ribbon. A Dremel Moto-Tool or high-speed jeweler's drill is used for this. Using a jeweler's pliers or other handy tool, bend a piece of wire and clip off, leaving a small stem to be inserted into the hole. Apply a little glue to the stem before inserting it. Set this aside to dry for thirty minutes before using.

Carol Arnold is a friend of mine who is an artist, designer, and scrimshander. Getting her start in England where she graduated from art school, she found her way to Nantucket Island, Massachusetts, where her work has become most sought after. For many years summer tourists have been buying her jewelry, which is so much in demand that she can't keep up with the orders. Her work is distinctive in its young, delicate style, unlike the nautical themes most common to scrimshaw. Many of her contemporary pieces are designed with abstract and subtle designs. She has decorated bone purses, the ivory pieces for the famous Nantucket lightship baskets, snuffboxes, and more elaborate sculpture to wear.

Now living in a Soho loft in New York City, Carol is working on her paintings and etchings. However, having supported herself for so long from the sale of her scrimshaw, she continues to meet the demand for her work, which is sold through New York galleries as well as on Nantucket. The simple pendant that she created to share with us was designed so that a beginner can learn the craft of scrimshaw without too much difficulty.

Recipe Box

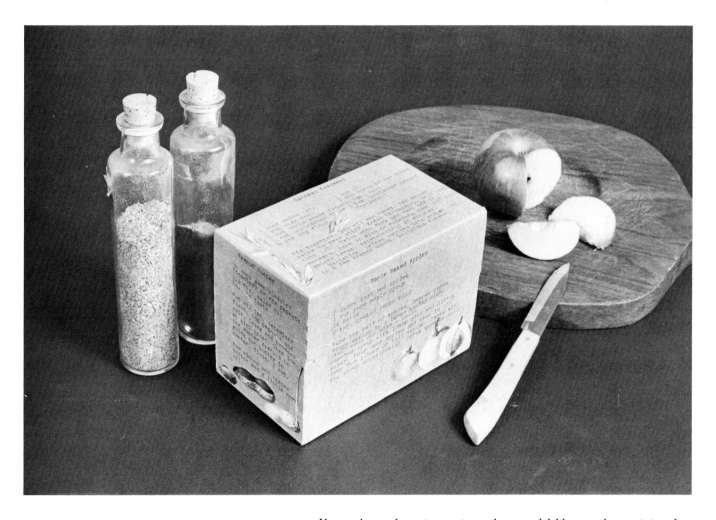

If you have favorite recipes that you'd like to share, it is often difficult to find a novel way to give them as a gift. Perhaps this recipe or file box will inspire you. The box is covered with kraft paper on which recipes have been typed. It's very easy to make, and if you have an old recipe box you can use it for this project. The box I used is made of wood and was purchased in an office supply store. Metal file boxes are easier to find and will work just as well. The crafting technique is decoupage simplified.

Materials needed are: file box for 3 x 5 file cards, brown kraft paper, Elmer's glue, pencil, scissors, simple cutout designs, spray varnish.

Begin by placing each side of the file box on the kraft paper and draw an outline so that you have five pieces. The bottom isn't covered. Cut out each piece. Select recipes that, when typed, will fit in the space provided by each piece. If you aren't sure, type the

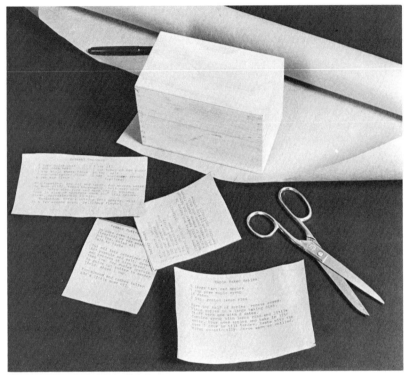

Recipes are typed on kraft paper.

recipes on plain paper first to determine which ones will fit. I chose recipes that could be illustrated easily. When typing the recipes, leave a space on one side, top or bottom, to add a cutout design or two. This project is often easier if you find the cutouts first. For instance, I have a book of fruits and vegetables and knew that I had the subjects in the appropriate size. I then chose the recipes that included the ingredients that I felt would look well. I wanted to use a recipe for making peanut butter because I had some great pictures of peanuts. However, it is not difficult to find inexpensive colorful books with the material you will need. Select delicate, rather than overwhelming, subjects to cut out. Use cuticle scissors for best results.

Place the cutouts on the paper patterns to determine how you will use them. If you dilute the glue slightly it will spread best. Cover one side of the box and place the corresponding paper exactly in place. If it is a little large, the excess can be trimmed with a razor blade. I found that the kraft paper was difficult to smooth down and used a butter knife to help push out trapped air bubbles.

Once all sides have been covered, add the cutout designs where planned. The inside of the box can be painted, lined with wallpaper,

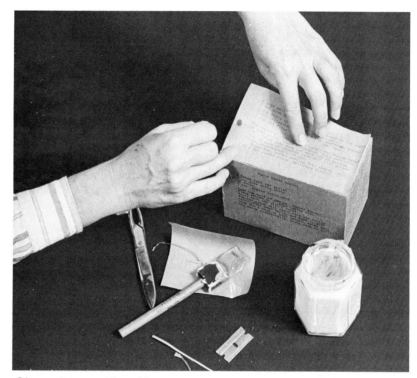

Glue recipes to sides of box.

kraft, or greeting paper, or you can leave it as is. Coat the entire outside with Krylon spray varnish. For the best results, hold the box about 12 inches away when spraying and keep the spray moving back and forth over the area. Do not overload or you will have drips and an uneven finish. Since the varnish dries in approximately twenty minutes, it is best to apply three thin coats rather than one very thick coating. Let each application dry thoroughly before reapplying.

Keep the top of the box slightly ajar with a toothpick, for instance, to keep it from sticking closed. Do not leave the top fully open as the varnish will drip while drying. If the surface is bumpy when completed, sand very lightly with a fine grit sandpaper or rub with #0000 steel wool. To add protection to the finished box, give it a coat of furniture wax.

If you are making this to give as a gift, you might want to add more recipes on the file cards inside. For an added touch, cut a piece of kraft paper large enough to wrap the box. Type recipes all over it before wrapping. Tie with a pink ribbon and add a cinnamon stick or a few bay leaves or other spices that might relate to your recipes.

Stenciled Sheet Set

A stencil is a thin plate or sheet of metal, leather, paper, or other material cut or pierced with a pattern or design. This is laid upon a surface and paint or ink is brushed or rubbed over it, thus leaving the basic color of the surface imprinted with the design or pattern cut out.

In the eighteenth and nineteenth centuries, stenciled designs were found in abundance in American farmhouses. Primarily used as a substitute for costly wallpaper, the designs were seen on walls as well as furniture and floors. These designs were often copied from the expensive wallpapers. Borders for the top of walls next to the ceiling were another popular and unusual way to personalize a room. Today we often think of the early American rockers and furniture displaying the designs of the Pennsylvania Dutch as stenciled furniture.

It is not difficult to make your own stencil, and applying a design to fabric doesn't require any special skills or talent. Sheets and pillowcases come in every color of the rainbow, but, as gifts go, they are not very exciting. The decorative sheets created by famous designers are often quite expensive. However, you can be your own designer by creating a personalized stencil.

Lou-Ann Luiz collects ducks. She has miniature ducks, soft, cuddly ducks, even a duck candle. All her friends know that ducks are Lou-Ann's favorite. We kidded her about having a college dorm room that looked like a nursery, but that doesn't faze her a bit. So it seemed only fitting that ducks should inhabit the borders of her sheet and pillowcase. She may even use the sheet as a bedspread. If you know someone with a particular interest you can make a simple stencil design for a similar project. However, the duck design could be used for any child's room, or perhaps you know a grownup who, like Lou-Ann, is a little kid at heart.

Acrylic paint is used for this project because it is permanent on fabric and can be washed in the washing machine and put in a dryer. This also means that it's a good idea to do this project away from a carpeted area as well as any upholstered furniture. Since the area to be stenciled is small, this shouldn't present a real problem.

The materials needed are: one blue cotton twin-size sheet, one matching pillowcase, stencil board (available in art stores), stipple brush or 1-inch flat paint brush, white acrylic paint, bright yellow or orange acrylic paint (small tubes), X-acto knife, a piece of tracing paper, embroidery thread to match yellow or orange paint, needle.

We are sticking to the most basic kind of stenciling because a simple design is the best way to begin. As you may know, stenciled objects can be extremely elaborate, delicate, complicated, and time

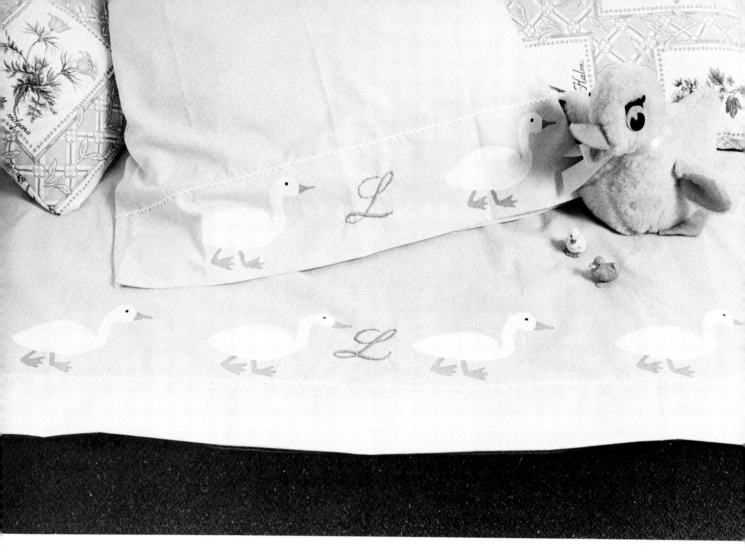

consuming to execute. The materials and tools that I have used for this project are basic and will get you started. They can be used for any stenciling project, simple or complicated. However, for more refined stenciling there are better tools which are simply more expensive versions of the basics. These too are available in art supply stores and you can consider buying them once you have tried the craft to see if you want to do more. I think it's good to know that you can actually do a professional-looking project before making a large investment.

Begin by making a tracing to use as your guide. Draw a straight line at the bottom of the paper. Trace the duck from the book twice. (Other designs are also provided.) There should be a 2½-inch space between the ducks, measuring between the bill of one and tail feathers of the other. If you are using another design be sure that it will fit on the object to be stenciled. Two ducks will be cut from the stencil board so that all of them will be spaced exactly the same distance apart. When stenciling a border design, it will be more accurate if the repeat pattern is cut from one board so they are spaced exactly the desired distance apart, as opposed to using one design that must be precisely measured and placed in position each time.

Transfer the tracing onto the stencil board. They should be close to but not touching the bottom edge of the board. Place the stencil board on a cutting board, and cut through the outline. To cut your

Trace design.

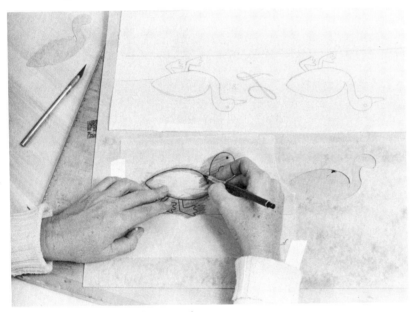

Transfer initial to be embroidered.

stencil use a very sharp X-acto knife blade. Cut out the body and head of both ducks. Save these cutout pieces. Since the bill and feet will be another color you will cut these areas away later.

To Cut Stencil

When cutting the design, incline the knife away from the center in order to bevel the edges. This will insure a clean, crisp outline, avoiding seepage of paint under the edges. The blade should be kept very sharp. Turn the paper as you cut.

Decide where on the sheet the stenciled ducks will be placed. If the hem is quite wide you might place them in this area. The sheet I used had a narrow hem, so the ducks fit better along the top of the seam line. Find the center of your sheet and tape the stencil in position so that the space between the ducks is over the center of the sheet. You will be working toward each outer edge. The embroidered initial will later be worked into the center area.

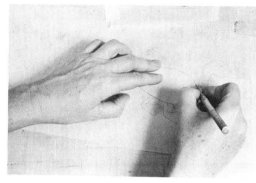

Cutting stencil with X-acto knife.

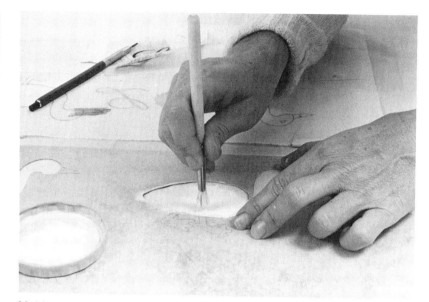

Hold stipple brush upright and tap up and down.

Replace body pieces while stenciling feet and bills.

Stenciling

For best results use a medium-sized stipple brush. Squirt a small amount of white paint into a shallow dish. When stippling, the brush should not be overloaded with paint. Hold the brush upright and tap up and down vigorously. If you are using a flat paint brush be sure to paint carefully from the outer edges to the center. The paint should not be too wet and the brush must be dry. Begin filling in the body area first so that most of the paint will be thinner when you reach the outer edges. Too much paint on the brush will create a smudged and uneven outline. Apply one thin coat, let this dry, and reapply, if necessary. Fill in the areas for both ducks before lifting the board and placing it down again. Work back and forth on each side until you reach the edges. In this way one duck can be drying while you work on the other side. Be sure to check yourself so that the ducks are always lined up correctly. Do this by placing one cutout stencil over an already painted duck before painting in the following one. Once all the bodies and heads have been painted, tape the cutout pieces back in position on the stencil board. This will protect your already stenciled areas while applying color to the bill and feet.

Cut out the remaining areas to be stenciled. Mix orange or yellow acrylic paint to the desired brilliance and stencil the bills and feet. Take care to be sure that everything is lined up correctly. A little time spent here will be well worth it. When the paint is dry, place a black dot for the eye on each duck's head. This can be done with a pointed artist's brush.

Embroidered Initial

Enlarge one of our script initials (on **page 61**) so that it is 1¾ inches high. Transfer it to the center of the sheet with pencil rubbing. I used a running satin stitch to embroider this. You might prefer to transfer one of the letters that incorporates a floral design. If so, be sure there is enough space between the ducks. The color you choose for the thread might match the orange of the bills and feet. Almost every color imaginable is available in embroidery thread.

The pillowcase is done the same way. Find the center (only the front of ours is done) and work toward the outer edges. Embroider an initial on the border of the pillowcase.

For a final touch, run a line of small white rickrack trim along the stitched hemline of the sheet and pillowcase.

When wrapping this gift you might include a stuffed duck. Wouldn't this make a perfect Easter present? Tuck a chocolate bunny under the ribbon.

If you do this project for your own child, consider extending the design further. The ducks might walk across window shades. Paint an unfinished dresser and stencil the ducks onto the drawers. And, for a variation, use one of our heart patterns to create another stencil. Red hearts on white sheets could make a young girl very happy.

Since this very basic kind of stenciling is so easy, unlike the intricate designs we often see on walls and floors, this project can be completed in a couple of hours. This is the kind of craft project that I like best. The end result is delightful and you don't have to learn complicated directions in order to do it. However, if you'd like to do more stenciling there are several books that will have you "oohing" and "ahing" over the designs.

Designs for stenciling.

Woven Name Banner

When working on a book containing general craft projects, I try to avoid the ones that everyone can't do. Any craft that requires instruction over a period of time in order to learn the technique should not be included. Equally, any craft which requires a large investment in special equipment. This usually means that the craftworker must make a commitment to the craft which goes far beyond creating one project. Crafts such as pottery, which must be done on a potter's wheel, or weaving projects, where a loom is essential, fall into this category, and I am always regretful for the elimination. However, the increased interest in weaving, for the beginner as well as professional, has given it a renewed position in the craft world, to the extent that a suggested weaving project might not be out of line.

Rene Rudjinsky is a young mother and weaver. At home in her apartment her loom is very much a central factor in her life. With a baby at home she spends much time creating new ideas to be expressed through her weaving. "Actually, I do most of my weaving at night," she confesses. "Do you know how impossible it is to work with a two-year-old interrupting every other second?" In her hallway an exciting wall hanging is on display, but I was more interested in the name banners she had woven for her children's bedroom. I have included them here as an idea because it is Rene's own design and the subtle colors and delightful characters are so appealing. Rene says this must be woven on a loom, and you should have some knowledge of weaving as this is not a beginner's project.

The banners measure 64 inches long and 10 inches wide. Each square is 8 x 10 inches. The rounded letters are Rene's adaptation of those found in many children's elementary or coloring books. She prefers Candide wool because of the wide range of colors, although for this she used only four colors: burnt orange, mustard, marine blue, and white. The warp is four-ply cotton and the ends are five to an inch.

She began by making a sketch, then designed the individual squares to size in order to follow her design accurately while weaving. The characters were adapted from children's books.

Since Adam is always right at his mother's elbow when she is weaving he feels that this is just as much his project. While Jon set up the camera, Adam was busy assembling all his friends for the picture.

Detail of banner.

Woven hanging by Rene Rudjinsky.

Stuffed Strawberry Pillows

When I first met Georgia McGurl, about eight years ago, she was already beyond the hobby stage with her craft. I would often come across her appliqué pillows, aprons, and soft sculpture in specialty boutiques or on display at a craft fair. Occasionally I would open the newspaper and there she'd be. Aside from being a beautiful subject for a photographer, her craftwork has attracted much local attention. "It's really fun to be paid for what I enjoy doing best," says Georgia. Like Carol Davis and JoAnn Carbonier, who make the appliqué T-shirts, Georgia has terrific working arrangements. With school-age children she can control her hours and output. Although she has a comfortable, sunny workroom, like most craft people, Georgia's work can't be contained. Every room boasts evidence of Georgia McGurl's existence. A basket filled with fabric sits in a corner of the bedroom, a drawer left open reveals appliquéd shirts, and soft, stuffed Christmas ornaments fill the breakfast area. Each room is personally stamped with Georgia's creative input. Even the bathroom is dominated by a huge, stuffed flower. They are infectious. I want them all: stuffed, luscious pink strawberries; a yellow calico pear, and butterflies with plump, graceful wings. "They aren't difficult to make. I can cut a pattern for you in a second. They are made from one basic shape, then stylized," she explains, while cutting a pattern for a strawberry pillow. "This is probably the best shape for people to start with." Besides, who doesn't love strawberries?

"I just finished making a bunch of pillows for a friend. She had ordered calico in different colors for a quilt that would go on her daughter's bed. She asked me to make pillows using the different calico fabric on each shape. This made the room that much more personalized."

Georgia also makes little strawberry sachets which she says are fun to make in bunches. These are filled with a potpourri for sweet-smelling baby strawberries. The pattern shown can be used same size for the miniature sachets, but must be scaled up for the pillow which measures 11 inches long and 13½ inches across at the widest section.

Whether you are making a sachet or pillow you will need the following materials: a piece of white chalk, scissors, needle and thread, fiber fill for stuffing, ½-yard fabric for pillow body, small scraps for sachets, ½-yard green velveteen or corduroy for leaves and stem.

When selecting fabric, Georgia suggests calico, gingham, or a tiny print in red or pinky colors. Avoid using solids, as this will be boring. An overall tiny print is more interesting. The stem and leaves are cut from a plush, textured material, or, if you prefer, these can be cut from a green calico, for instance.

Hold your pattern piece on the fabric with one hand while drawing around the outline with white chalk. Cut two pieces. With right sides together stitch around the strawberry, leaving a 3½-inch opening at the top. Clip the edges before turning inside out.

Cut two pieces for the stem in the same way. The strawberry pillow has five leaves, so you will need ten leaf pieces. With right sides of the stem pinned together, stitch around edges, leaving an opening at the bottom where it will be joined to the body. Stitch each of the leaves in this way, leaving a 1½-inch opening at the side of one point. Turn right side out and press.

Next, stuff the pillow with fiber fill, which you can get in a fabric shop. Stuff the stem in the same way and stitch across the bottom. With needle and thread gather the opening around the top of the strawberry so there is enough room to stuff the end of the stem into the opening. Then stitch the stem to the body.

Stuff each of the leaves with the fiber fill so they are full, but not too plump. Slip-stitch the opening of each leaf closed. Set your sewing machine for a basting stitch and run the machine down the center of each leaf as though you were quilting it. This is the vein. The stitches should stop short of the tip on each leaf. Stitch the leaves to the stem, pushing them down as close to the body as possible.

Georgia cutting a calico strawberry pattern.

Stuff and stitch leaves for pillow.

Strawberry Sachets

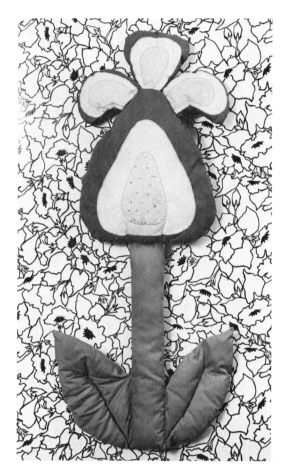

When cutting the pattern for the sachet, the body and stem are made the same way as the pillow, just smaller. However, when stuffing the body you will fill it three-quarters full of fiber. The rest is a mixture of long-grain rice, ground cloves, cinnamon, and one drop of strawberry oil.

The leaves are cut with pinking shears and are not stuffed. Georgia thinks ribless corduroy or velvet, or felt work best. She draws veins on each leaf, using a black ball-point pen. Do not use markers, as they will bleed on the fabric.

Georgia uses the sachets as Christmas ornaments or to sweeten a closet. For hanging, cut a 2½-inch piece of satin or grosgrain ribbon, fold it in half, and stitch at the opening near the base of the stem. Tack each of the leaves around the stem. Make many in different calico prints for a handmade country look to decorate a small Christmas tree.

Pictured here are further examples of Georgia McGurl's appliqué and soft sculpture work.

78

Wood Type Assemblage

Early American typesetters used wooden type for large head-lines, posters, displays, etc. As new technology took over, the old wooden type fonts were burned or discarded to make way for the new equipment. Much of it has found its way into secondhand stores, antique shops, or still sits in the drawers of old typesetting or printing firms. Today it has become a favorite creative devise of artists, designers, and decorators.

The type would get dirty and smooth from constant use. Over the years they took on a dark patina that varies from type to type. The different shades make it that much more interesting. Considered true antiques, the era of wood-type manufacturing flourished briefly and disappeared quickly, leaving little written record of its designers and manufacturers, except for scattered personal accounts and specimen catalogs.

Returning from a business trip to Australia, Dan McGurl brought with him a suitcase full of the wooden printer's type. From this magnificent horde he was able to put together an unusually well-designed wood assemblage. All typeface is a particular size and style, so it is remarkable to realize that this assemblage is made up of words, places, and particular interests of the McGurl family, as well as the names of Georgia, Dan, and their children. To do this, Dan had to have about ten times the type needed to make the actual names, using letters that are the same size. For instance, if he had 3-inch high narrow gothic he would need enough of them in the right letters. This assemblage takes a lot of patience to get everything fitting well and designed artistically. Dan McGurl's is a magnificent example of a wood type assemblage.

The three-dimensional effect of such a project is achieved because type is .918 inches deep, or, in printer's terms, type high. This is just under an inch, affording a chunkiness to the overall look. The quality of the woods that were used to make the type adds to the richness of the art. Most of the wood type was made from cherry, maple, apple, or pine.

Once the basic design was created, Dan put it together, set in a wooden frame. This assemblage is very heavy and must be carefully hung. It would not help to show someone making such a project as the arrangement depends entirely on the type you find. Often it is possible to come across one letter which can be used alone or with other decorative pieces that can create a grouping on a wall. You might have to settle for different typefaces in order to create your name or a word.

Since the wood type was used for printing, the letters are all backwards. One printer we know mounted his name in type on the door to his office. He used the letters to print his name on the wall behind the door. When the door is opened it appears as though the name has just been printed there.

Embroidered Mittens

Children love to have their names on everything. Mothers like this too because it makes it easier to identify in the school lost-and-found. This is especially true when it concerns hats, mittens, and sneakers.

For fun I bought a pair of inexpensive mittens for one of my favorite little girls. Using a darning needle and several different colored yarns, I quickly and easily embroidered her name. This is a simple satin stitch which is obviously not as refined as embroidery done with cotton embroidery thread. However, the wool stitches have a crude charm. There isn't any planning involved, just a haphazard design. Each letter is a different color and the project can be done in less than an hour.

Initials and names can decorate wool caps and scarves in this colorful way as well. If you would prefer, plan a design on paper, then copy it as a yarn painting onto the mittens. You can even teach a child to do his or her own, which might be all the more fun. For added detail make crisscrosses of each different thread color around the cuffs. They will look like little snowflakes.

Fantasy Photo

A family party is always cause for taking snapshots and occasionally one or two are especially good. Often they are tucked away once everyone has shared the first joy of seeing them. Sometimes they are stuck in an album, and only enjoyed again when the family gathers.

My sister's son, Judd, is seven and has a motorized truck that is this year's passion. The picture of him as king of the road deserved an elaborate setting, so we created one. You could design your own background by tracing any picture from a coloring book or similar source. However, the design provided here is adaptable for a variety of uses. Place any child on the colorful fantasy road which has been designed to fit an 8 x 10-inch frame.

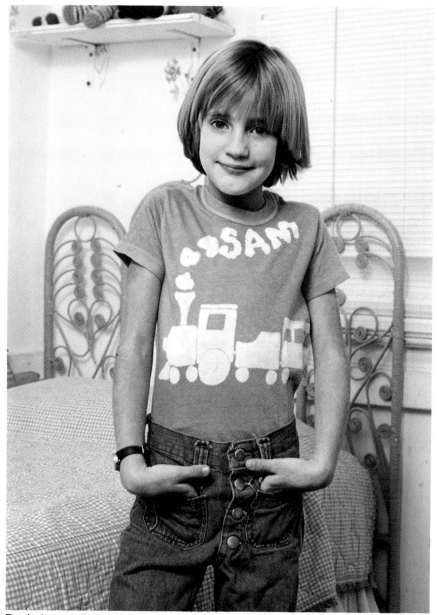

Batik design, Karen Kalkstein

Recipe box

Heart pockets

Beach bag, Lisa Brunhuber

Needlepoint design, Harriet Doniger

Stenciled ducks

Appliquéd T-shirt, Carol Davis

Grandmother pillow, Ann Laredo

Embroidered child's sheet

Collector's bag, Ruth Linsley

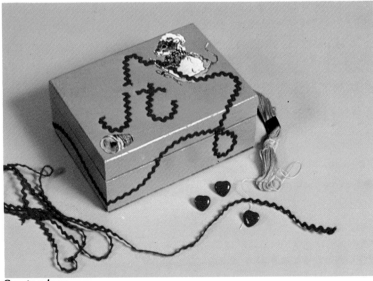

Sewing box

Strawberry pillows, Georgia McGurl

Xerox transfer shirts

Rebecca Ellsley's gingerbread house

Holiday gift bag

Christmas stocking

Party tray

Address oval

Tennis party table setting, Louise Coe

Table setting, Louise Coe

Trace and transfer design to illustration board.

Materials needed are: a snapshot, scissors, several colorful water-soluble markers or colored pencils, a black permanent marker, heavy white paper, tracing paper, 8 x 10-inch frame, glue.

Trace the design shown here, or another of your choice. Transfer the design onto heavy white paper. This is easily done by rubbing pencil over the back of the entire design. Turn the paper right side up, lay it on the white paper, and, with a ball-point pen, retrace the outline. Using the black permanent marker go over the outline that you have just transferred.

The next step is easy and will remind you of kindergarten days. Water-soluble markers can be purchased in art supply and stationery stores and come in a variety of bright colors. A small box contains enough of a selection to do any project. If you prefer, colored pencils can be used. Color in the picture by following our suggestion or simply doing it the way you think it would look best. Ours is very bold and bright.

Cut away any excess paper around the figure in the snapshot and glue in place on the road. Spread the glue to the outer edges of the photograph and press down with your palm. Any excess glue

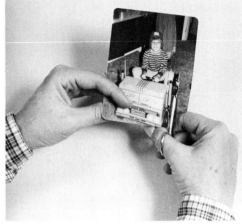

Cut figure from snapshot.

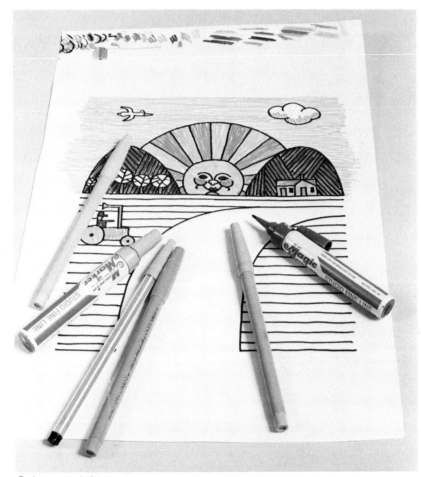

Color in with Magic Markers or crayons.

that oozes out can be easily removed with a slightly damp sponge. We used a plastic box frame, but the inexpensive frames are fine. You might even find an elaborate or unusual frame for your photograph.

If you want to do more of this kind of project, consider finding different scenes and taking snapshots for the particular scene. Think of unusual poses that could work with the people you will be photographing. If someone is learning to ski, for instance, you might create a very steep and winding mountain as a backdrop, although the photo is taken of the person standing still on flat ground.

Table Settings with Pzazz!

I always thought table settings were either fairly conventional or full-blown *House Beautiful* affairs. If you are like most people, you don't have a variety of china and silverware that materializes for different occasions. And the only people who seem to entertain with beautiful extravagance are those pictured in the magazines, usually celebrities. "Not true," states my friend Louise Coe, emphatically. When Louise sets a table it is sensational and her guests can't figure out how she does it over and over again. Louise has a very definite philosophy about setting an exquisite table and agreed to share some of her ideas with us.

"To begin with," she says, "your table should look no less than a knockout. When your guests walk into your dining room they should know they're at a party." Sometimes Louise uses a theme, sometimes a color; often she fills the table with things that she finds interesting or pleasing to look at. Guests are always enthusiastic over Louise's settings because she believes in taking the time necessary to make it look as good as she possibly can. "Your table is a reflection of you. As a hostess your table should be as impressive as the food. After all," she continues, "if you take care to prepare delicious food and you plan what you will wear and how well you want to look, your table should be given the same attention."

As a former model and interior designer, Louise also worked as a fashion coordinator in New York City. Her style, sophistication, and good taste are reflected in everything she does, paying meticulous attention to details. Dressing a table is another of her creative expressions. Louise, Jerry, and their son, Mark, have a very casual life-style and this is also considered when preparing for a party. Louise feels that if you plan carefully, leaving yourself plenty of time, you and your guests will enjoy yourselves that much more. It takes time to do anything well and often people underestimate the importance of a well-designed table.

Louise suggests beginning with color. You might start with your tablecloth. It isn't necessary to restrict yourself to conventional tablecloths. An interesting piece of fabric, even a cotton Indian bedspread, can be exciting and set the stage for everything to follow. Louise found a printed spread that she especially likes because of the colors and design. "The whimsical animal print is humorous and can become a conversation piece. I always like to inject a bit of humor in my settings," she adds. This is another aspect to Louise's personality and makes her tables that much more entertaining. One of the predominant colors in the fabric is dusty pink, which she will try to emphasize in the rest of the setting. If you have pretty china, you might pick out one of the colors in the pattern to exaggerate

Louise Coe

and make a focal point. Next take stock of what you have around your home. Consider glasses, plates, placemats, napkins, etc. You might buy some cloth napkins to have in your favorite colors; or all one color; or many different colors. If you are setting the table around one color, carry it through all the way. For instance, if you put mints on a green table, take the trouble to find green mints and put them in a contrasting green tin or interesting holder that picks up the color.

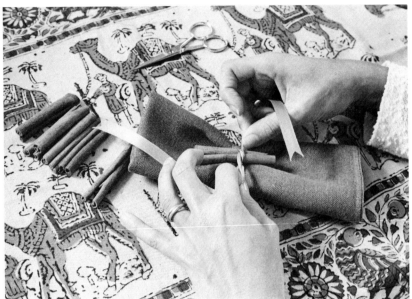

Tuck cinnamon sticks under the bow.

A gourd is used as a name tag.

Each place setting can be a complete and separate unit, while being integrated as part of the overall look. For example, Louise likes to find unusual things to amuse her guests. She has a collection of Lucky Strike tins that pick up the pink and green colors of the tablecloth. She may use one or two at one person's place. These can be filled and become functional, or they might be used for display. A framed baby picture can add humor and will surely be something to talk about. African violets are another of Louise's favorites; the pink buds and green leaves once more accenting her colors. "People don't usually think of putting plants on the table. They will use cut flowers, overlooking an interesting possibility," she says. Put a plant off to one side, not necessarily in the middle of the table. You might add candles here and there, again picking up the color you are using. Maybe two candles placed together at the edge of one place setting would be fitting.

Table setting, Louise Coe.

Aside from the visual considerations, Louise thinks about smell. Food smells are important, but the more subtle scents of spices are great when included in the settings. For one of Louise's tables she uses cinnamon sticks tied with delicate pink-satin ribbon around a cinnamon-colored napkin. The pink is the exact color of the African violet, and quietly picks up the colors in her tins and table covering.

If you are having more than four people you can add name tags at each setting. Louise thinks that a party of six to eight people is comfortable because you can talk to everyone and individuals can visit with each other as well. For a very small party, names at places seem too formal, but for a large party this is a good idea, to create ease when being seated. For a Thanksgiving table you might use gourds or squash to identify each guest's place. Use black marker to outline each name. If it fits with your color scheme, try writing on bananas!

When everything looks just right, stand back and survey the whole effect. Then throw in something zany. Louise says she always tries to find something totally inappropriate, something that definitely doesn't belong. It is a foil and adds that bit of humor. She also recommends including something either black or white no matter what colors you have used. "It cuts the richness and takes away from a contrived look. It's kind of like adding a touch of vanilla to chocolate brownies. It refreshens." This might be a clear, crystal salt

Tennis party setting.

shaker filled with white salt. Black candles are terrific, even black napkins. Sometimes Louise sets a totally black-and-white table. In this case you wouldn't add any color. It should be like a black-and-white photograph with no color to spoil the effect.

Last summer Louise helped a friend create an after-tennis party table. I asked her to re-create one setting to demonstrate a completely different look. Louise is a very close friend and while I adore her, I had to work hard to keep an open mind when she plopped a big (but clean) sneaker on the table. Next she slipped a short water glass into a striped athletic sock and placed this in the sneaker. "A little craziness adds to any occasion," she assured me. The white laces were replaced by bright red ones and the glass was filled with pink geraniums for more color. The paper tablecloth carries out the red, white, and blue color scheme and Louise often uses a placemat on top of the table covering. In this case she used red-and-white paper placemats with bold ENJOY across them.

Bon voyage name tag.

Wheat tucked under a ribbon for fall.

Next she looked through her linen drawer and chose stark-white napkins. Plates with a blue pattern were perfect. ''The colors needn't match exactly,'' she adds, adjusting a turquoise water glass. ''My antique sports tin is the same color as the glass. That works well.'' She's inspired to place a tennis book under the sneaker for a little more excitement, the type being red, white, and blue. ''This person can read if the party gets boring,'' she teases.

Every detail is given careful consideration as she places a white spoon where something is needed. It is as though she's creating a beautifully executed still-life painting. And her guests always appreciate her efforts. The final touch is a yellow tennis ball inscribed with a black marker. Isn't this a delight?

Some additional suggestions Louise offers are name tags for a bon voyage party, a sprig of wheat under a brown ribbon for the celebration of fall. Almost any excuse can be used for a party. If you are planning to buy something, consider an offbeat color and have a dozen of whatever it is. It might be shocking pink wine glasses, purple napkins, or chartreuse plates. Always combine texture on your table such as tin, glass, straw, linen, crystal, and baskets.

Louise Coe recommends two things that she feels are most important to insure success. Everything you put on your table should be absolutely sparkling clean. No matter what it is, it must be clean. Besides the dishes, silverware, napkins, and tablecloth, which we take for granted, wash out the little mint tin, clean the glass of your picture frame, and, of course, wash the sneaker before using it. Next take special care to make your guests feel comfortable. Don't overload each place. Make sure that each person has plenty of room, doesn't feel cramped, and has an unobstructed view for conversing with the other guests.

After a day of setting tables, Louise and Jerry and Jon and I sat down for a casual dinner. Nothing fancy, no preplanning, just good food, good friends, relaxed conversation . . . the basic ingredients.

Party Tray

When my children were small the biggest event in their lives was a birthday party. It was always a lot of fun to create a pretty table and to think of prizes that the children would enjoy winning. One of my children was born in August, and it always seemed appropriate to have an outdoor picnic party. For this I devised a party tray with each child's name personalizing his or her place setting. This project might take a bit of time, depending on the number of children attending the party, and should therefore be made well in advance. However, it is well worth the time spent and can be very handy for a barbecue where each child gets his or her own food. For gift giving, make one for each child in the family to use for everyday.

The tray is made from Grumbacher's Stretchtite foldup paper canvas made for paintings. It is made of heavy white textured paper. Intended for easy hanging, I have reversed it, using the back of it as a tray. Since it has punch-out holes for hanging, these spaces are perfect for holding lollipops.

The materials needed are: 9 x 12-inch Hypro Stretchtite (available in art supply stores), selection of acrylic paint colors, tube of white acrylic paint, 1-inch paint brush, stencil brush, stencil letters, glossy spray varnish.

The acrylic paints are very intense in color and can be used as is or mixed to the desired shades. The canvas is scored for folding and therefore gives you a guideline when painting the stripes. A stiff

Paint different-colored stripes on the canvas.

brush is best for this. It is not necessary to be exact when painting each stripe. However, leave a thin strip of white between each paint color. When the paint dries, plan the spacing of each name. Stencil letters come in various sizes, and if you have a very long name it will require smaller letters in order to fit in the space. If you want to use the large capital letters and the name is long, consider placing each letter at random so that the name goes up and down.

Place the stencil sheet in position on the tray and tap the white paint onto the letter space. Do this repeatedly until the area is covered. For a clear, sharp letter it is best to put a small amount of

Stencil on flat canvas before folding.

Fold tray after stenciled letters are dry.

Protect finished project with varnish.

paint on at a time, going over the area with your brush in an upright position. Let each letter dry before continuing.

Fold the Stretchtite up on the sides where indicated and tuck in the flaps to form the tray. Paint the edges with a bright color.

Spray the entire project with glossy spray varnish. This will dry in about twenty minutes, and if you want added protection repeat with another coating. The varnish will make the paper tougher and waterproof for many usings. It will also give the tray a shiny finish.

Select lollipops in the paint colors and poke them into the pre-punched holes around the rim. I always like to use M & M's because they are the rainbow colors of the paint. Balloons, hats, and napkins can also be in the paint colors used.

Inspired by the place settings created by my friend Louise Coe, I tried to find some unusual ideas for further dressing up the table. The paper tablecloths found in party shops seem to clash with the bold party trays. A piece of fabric might be used or, in this case, linen dish-towel fabric. It is inexpensive and can be purchased by the yard. Great for absorbing spills, later to be washed and used again. A contrasting fabric is used for the napkins. In the long run this is more practical than the paper goods, which are expensive and can only be used once. Another suggestion is to buy different-colored washcloths to replace napkins. Tie each one with a ribbon and a prize tucked within. A variety of five-and-ten toys or novelties can also be used as decoration and will amuse the children while sitting at the table.

Alphabet Needlepoint

A good way to create an original needlepoint design might be to follow the example of Ann Laredo. Ann creates her own free-form designs within the highly structured form of a letter. The "A" pillow is one of her designs that she plans and paints before committing it to the canvas. Her beautifully painted letters show how she balances color and form, but always keeping the design within the outline of the initial. Once Ann gets going, her confidence often allows her to change the design in midstream, if inspired to do so. You can see an example of this in the "L" pattern, comparing it to the actual work. Her miniature pillows are made to order and are always the size of the letter, keeping the emphasis on the design. Ann has a good feeling for proportion and suggests that this is an excellent project to experiment with a design that you create according to your taste. You might try an Indian design or Art Deco done in black-and-white yarn. Ann's pillow backgrounds are kept solid to further emphasize the strong, graphic design of the letter.

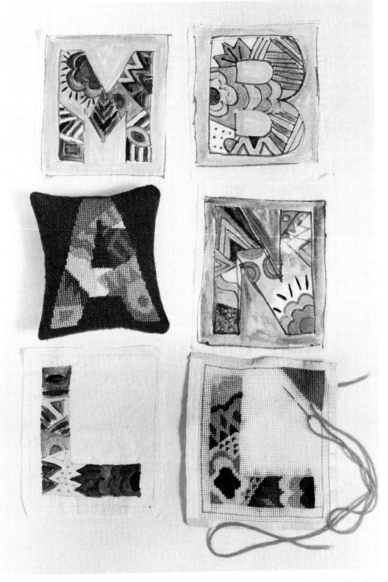

Ann Laredo owns the Sunflower shop, where she sells her many original creations; among them: whimsical papier-mâché animals and fruit, painted wicker baskets, and, her most noted, faux-painted (simulated antique) furniture. Receiving her art training at Cooper Union in New York, Ann's education and talent have contributed to a never-ending source of creative enthusiasm. There is almost no area of crafts that she hasn't experimented with.

Sunflower's walls are a burst of exciting, colorful paintings, confirming the fact that there is a bit of fantasy in all of Ann's work. The orders for her initialed needlepoint pillows keep her busy long after Sunflower closes for the day. "I'm always working on something, whether it's in the shop or at home," she says. Interior decorators are familiar with Ann's work and call for her services often. One day she may be sponge stippling a delicate, antique chair; the next day, constructing a dollhouse; and the next week, putting the finishing touches on a painting.

Most of the work in Sunflower is hers, and the diversity of good design and craftmanship is apparent. Ann Laredo is a fine example of today's working woman who has used her good business sense to market her talents successfully, while also raising a family.

Grandmother Pillow

The small appliquéd pillow is a gift that Ann Laredo designed to give to grandmothers. Of course nobody is excluding mothers, and this would be a beautiful baby celebration present. Consider filling it with fiber and potpourri for a sweet-scented bed pillow. Ann achieves a delicate quality with the use of pale pastel, organdy, and lace.

The designs provided here can be traced and transferred to scraps of fabric. A cat might be cut from pink gingham to which you will add pale green embroidered detail. Arrange the appliqués in an overall pattern on the front of the heart-shaped background material. Stitch them with a zigzag machine or satin-stitch by hand. Each child's name is then added with machine stitching or embroidery. If desired, include the birth date of each child.

Valentine Surprise

February is a love month. It is a time to send valentine greetings to long-forgotten friends. You can really go overboard for Valentine's Day without breaking the bank, and if you've tired of the traditional cards why not send a surprise valentine message? A felt-covered, foam rubber, over-sized valentine is folded and stuffed into a plastic photo cube. The valentine will completely fill the cube and must be carefully folded in order to squeeze it into the container. When opened, the receiver will get a surprise as the valentine pops out to full size.

You will need: ¼-yard of red felt (54 inches wide), a small piece of white felt, Spra-Ment fabric adhesive, ¼-inch thick 16½ x 17½-inch piece of foam rubber, scissors, plastic photo cube.

Trace one of the heart patterns and scale it up to size. It should measure slightly larger than 16½ inches across at the fattest part and 17½ inches long. Use the entire ¼-yard of fabric. Stitch around the outline, leaving a 2-inch opening to turn the heart inside out. Cut a piece of foam rubber slightly smaller than the heart pattern so that it will fit inside the felt. Slip-stitch the opening closed. A small white felt square, sold in fabric shops, is used for the letters. Trace each letter and transfer it to the felt. Cut these out. Spray the back with Spra-Ment fabric adhesive. Lay each letter in place in the center of the red felt and press down with the palm of your hand.

Fold the heart, slip it into the plastic photo cube, wrap it up in a plain brown wrapper, and send to your loved one.

100

Plexiglas Picture Frames

The kitchen table was laden with Plexiglas projects of all sizes and shapes; some, familiar objects, others, free-form whatever-you-want-to-call-them objects. "My family can't stand the stuff," admitted Don Hornung, not at all concerned about his family's indifference to his hobby. "Actually, they just don't like plastic. Oh, some of my tables are appreciated, but my free-form bowls have been super flops around here. Take this," he says, reaching into the cabinet and handing me a waffle-shaped affair that looks like a melted record. And before I can turn around, he's darting into another room to bring out more things. Frames in all sizes and shapes, bowls, a desk set, even a bagel holder. Don Hornung overflows with energy and enthusiasm for everything he does, which explains how a man who travels for part of every week, plays

tennis every chance he gets, and is a devoted family man can still find time to develop a hobby that began as an accident. "It relaxes me," he confesses.

Don is in the aluminum extrusion business, and when his company had an excess of scrap Plexiglas used for storm windows he knew he could find a use for it. As an inveterate tinkerer, he knew that something would develop in his home workshop. Now, just three years later, every cupboard in the house abounds with his Plexiglas creations. Down in the basement I was treated to a Plexiglas explosion. Everything was housed in clear plastic holders.

Measure and make pencil mark on paper backing.

Stacks of Plexi in varying shapes and colors stood waist-high on the floor. A huge display, spelling out the word NOEL, was in the process of Christmas readiness. "If I really get mad at anyone in the family," Don said humorously, "I threaten to put this on the front lawn." A giant twisted sculpture "happening" was discreetly stuck in the back of the room. There is almost nothing that Don hasn't or won't try with Plexiglas, and he keeps a notebook with drawings and plans for new ideas that he adds and refers to often. He cuts out pictures from catalogs in order to duplicate or improve on the items that he hasn't made before. The expensive Lucite or Plexiglas gift items that are so popular today can be made for a fraction of the cost, and Don says it isn't at all difficult.

Don learned his craft by reading a few good books on the subject and investing in some basic tools, which he uses to make all his projects. This is a good idea in the beginning, and later, when you feel that you'd like to go on with this craft, you can add to your supplies. "I've bought a few things that really aren't necessary, but are fun to have. A basic item, though, is the heating unit for bending the plastic. It is inexpensive and readily available in craft stores. This is needed for even the simplest projects, such as picture frames." A frame, says Don, is a good first project, since it is something that everyone can use, is easy to make, and takes only about a half hour. You'll probably want to make many after the first one.

Transfer signature to back of Plexi.

Cut through backing with X-acto knife.

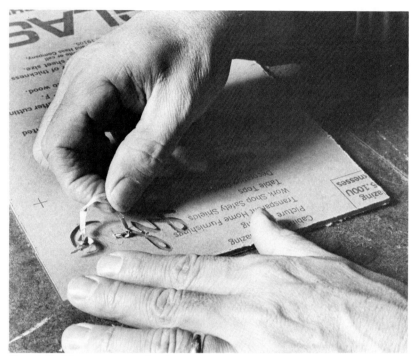
Carefully lift away paper backing.

The materials needed for an 8 x 11-inch frame are: a sheet of clear plastic 8 x 24 inches, heating strip element, saber saw (if sheet of plastic is not exact size), hacksaw blade, X-acto knife, spray paint, pencil.

Clear sheets of plastic are available in craft shops and from plastic dealers. Some manufacturers may even sell scrap pieces, so check your local Yellow Pages for suppliers. There are many brand names, the two most popular being Plexiglas, made by Rohm & Haas, and Lucite, made by Dupont. The plastic comes with a paper backing that is peeled away after it has been cut to the proper size. This paper protects the plastic from scratches while storing and cutting. Craft shops carry plastic cutters, which enable you to score and break the plastic, eliminating the use of a saw. However, this is not as easy to do, and if you have a saber or jigsaw, or, even better, a table saw, you will have no trouble getting a smooth cut. Don recommends the use of goggles when sawing the plastic.

The frame we made is 8 x 11 inches. However, you should customize yours to the size of your photograph. If your frame will measure 11 inches from top to bottom, you will need an extra 10½ inches to fold over and 2½ inches to fold back for the stand. The photograph is held between the two sections of Plexi.

Begin by measuring 8 inches across and 24 inches down. Draw a straight line where you will make your cut. Steady the saw and cut along your measured lines as carefully as possible. The edges of the cut Plexi are not smooth and will need buffing. If you have a well-equipped home workshop, you can use a buffing attachment on a drill. However, the back of a hacksaw blade will achieve the same effect. Using the dull edge, scrape the blade along the edges on an angle to get a beveled edge. If you place the piece of Plexi in a vise you will have both hands free to do this.

Measure down 10½ inches from the top to determine where the front fold will go. Make a pencil mark on the side edge. Next decide where you will want the name on the front. This will depend on the size of the photograph and where it will be placed in the frame. The name can be centered on the bottom or top, or placed in either corner. It should be spaced where it will look best. Lay the photograph on top of the front of the Plexi to determine this before proceeding. We used Don's daughter Lynn's signature for the lettering on this frame. However, on another frame Don used press-on plastic letters that can be purchased in art supply stores. The signature is first written on tracing paper. Thicken the letters so that there is approximately ¼-inch double line. Lay the tracing down so that it reads backwards and transfer it to the back of the Plexi. This is done on the paper side of the Plexiglas. Using an X-acto knife, cut through the outline of the signature. Carefully lift away the paper backing. Select the paint color of your choice and spray paint over the name that you have just created. Let this dry and recoat if necessary.

Peel all the paper backing away from the strip of Plexiglas before proceeding. Preheat your heating-strip element as directions indicate. Lay the piece of Plexi across the heat strip at the exact points you have marked on the sides, indicating 10½ inches from the top. Leave this for about three minutes. Do not overheat, as bubbles will form in the plastic. You can test to see if it is ready by bending the plastic slightly. If not, leave for another minute or two, keeping careful watch. Fold so that the extra piece comes over the front and press the two pieces of Plexi together. You can clamp them while the plastic is cooling. If you prefer, you can lay it on a table and place a board on top or hold with your hands until cool.

The second bend creates a stand for the frame. Measure 2½ inches from the bottom and lay the Plexi across the heating strip. When hot enough, fold this piece slightly, then place on a table and bend the top part of the frame back until it is at an angle that holds well. Hold this for a few seconds until it is cool.

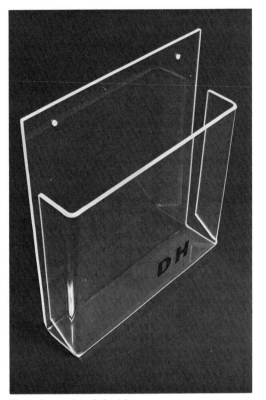

Telephone book holder.

Heat Plexi in order to bend it.

Fold Plexi in half to create the frame.

Clamp or hold in place until cool.

Make another fold for frame stand.

The photograph can now be slipped between the folded plastic, or you might like to make a mat border. For the smaller frame we used two different pieces of wallpaper to create an interesting background for Lynn's photograph.

Once you make a frame you will realize how easy it is to work with this material and you'll probably want to make other things. One of my favorite items that Don has made is a telephone book holder that fits on the inside of a kitchen cabinet door. It is made from one piece of Plexiglas which is bent and curved so that the book fits perfectly. Like all of Don's projects it is clean, simple, and neat. Everything that is held in Plexiglas containers is visible but out of the way. Aside from clear, this material comes in an opaque finish and can be purchased in a variety of colors. One of Don's more romantic endeavors was a transparent red heart on which he used press-on letters to write a message. It hangs in a window proclaiming, ''I Love You, Cissy.'' Another original Don Hornung idea is a grow stick. Each child's name is written by his or her notch, both engraved in the plastic by using a Dremel Moto-Tool, which is available in craft and toy stores. This is a handy tool to own, as you can use it for this and many other craft projects.

Photo Valentine

Use party apron heart pattern for this.

Because we liked the heart that Don made for his wife, Cissy, we asked him to demonstrate how easy it is to cut out a heart, using the Plexiglas. Next we enlarged a 35-mm color transparency and transferred it to the heart for an inexpensive, clever valentine gift.

Don suggests that it is no more difficult to cut out a shape than a straight line, if you follow your outline carefully. For this project use a translucent white Plexiglas. You can make the heart shape as large as you want. However, a slide can be blown up to a size of 8½ x 11 inches, so your heart should be no larger.

To do this project you will need access to a copy center that has a color Xerox machine. These centers are opening all over the country and most copy, photostat, or printing places have them. You can use any slide that you would like to transfer onto the heart. The slide fits into the color Xerox machine and can reproduce it on a wax backing to any size you want. This will look like a color Xerox blowup of your original slide. Lay the plastic heart in position on the Xerox and hold it up to a window or light to see how it will look. Adjust the picture as desired and tape it on each side to hold it in place.

Set your iron so that it is quite hot. Place a piece of silver foil over the back of the paper. The front of the heart is down on the ironing board. The foil will prevent the paper from scorching. Apply pressure and heat to the back of the photo. This will fuse the transfer photo to the plastic heart. Be sure to go over the entire area to be transferred. Turn the heart over and, with a razor blade, cut

away excess paper around the heart outline. Turn the heart face-down again and peel the paper backing away from the photo. The photo slide should be transferred onto the heart. When hung in a window, the light will shine through, turning the heart into an enlarged color slide of your favorite subject.

There are many shapes that can be cut from the Plexiglas and Don suggests experimenting with scraps of material to achieve different effects. The waffle-shaped bowls are made by placing a piece of Plexi in the oven until it begins to soften. Take it out and form the shape desired. "I even made an American flag out of different-colored pieces. They didn't like that either," Don says. Actually when Don is out of hearing range any member of his family will admit, "He's pretty good. But don't encourage him."

Enlarged transfer ready for mounting.

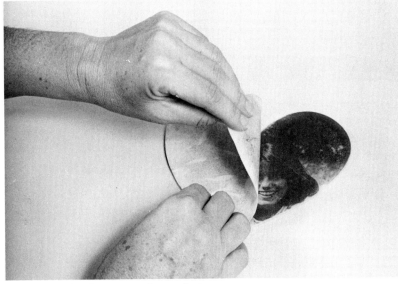

Tape plastic heart to Xerox transfer.

Peel paper backing away from photo.

Ribbons, Rickrack, and Embroidered Trimmings

Any plain shirt can be turned into a fanciful, personally designed gift with a little trimming expertise. The fabric shops carry ribbons, rickrack, calico trim, lace, buttons, and embroidery thread in every imaginable color and design. The addition of initialed and name tags, left over from camp and school labeling, can also be used. You can even make your own trimmings by cutting strips of various material. Add a few embroidered flowers, leaves, initials, or hearts and you have an interesting garment.

I chose this shirt because of the wide cuffs and outlined pocket. The red heart buttons replaced the white ones that matched the ones going down the front. I added one red button to each cuff as well. This shirt now has a peasant feeling, which is more charming than it was left plain. Experiment with different ideas before sewing the trims to the shirt.

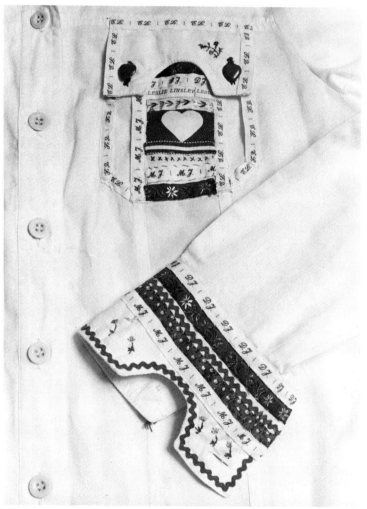

Personalized Appliquéd Emblem

It is not difficult to find a variety of appliqués for almost everyone's taste. However, if you have a special interest, or would like to stand out in the crowd, it is easy to design and make your own appliquéd emblem. Can your imagine the creative challenge of thinking up something really unique to make for a friend's special talent or interest.

Gary plays the harmonica, which seems like a good subject for a modern-looking appliquéd emblem to adorn a shirt. If you know someone who plays an instrument in a band this might be a way for him or her to personalize a performing outfit.

The harmonica is particularly nice because the design is ornate and can even be mistaken for just that—an ornate design. The fabric used for this is the silver nylon material that racing jackets are made from. It is sensational to paint on and sews on like a dream. This material comes in a gold color as well. You will need a very small piece, so buy as little as you can. Most shops insist on a ¼-yard minimum cut from a bolt, which is fine.

The materials needed are: silver nylon fabric, very fine black marker, variety of acrylic paint (small tubes), pointed artist's paint brush, cotton batting, sewing machine, pencil, tracing paper.

Trace the design shown here or one that you have found. It can be taken from a book, record album jacket, art and design annuals, packages or a photograph. Transfer the design onto the fabric. This is done by rubbing pencil over the back of the traced picture. Tape the design faceup on the nylon and go over the details of the outline with a ball-point pen.

Remove the tracing and go over the outline with a black marker. Using a pointed artist's brush, fill in the different areas with acrylic paint. If you are unsure about the color choice make a sketch first. Fill in the areas with colored markers or pencils so you can see how the finished project will look. Our design is color keyed. You can fill in lettering for a name or leave the space blank.

Cut a small rectangle of cotton batting so that it is the same size as the design. With this held in place on the back of the painted harmonica you will machine stitch around all black lines. This will quilt the appliqué, giving it a three-dimensional effect.

Next clip off the corners from the extra fabric and fold it toward the back. Press in place. Find the spot on your shirt where the appliqué will look best. Try it in different places before pinning it in place. Attach this to the shirt, using a slip stitch around the outer edge as close to the outline as possible. Press the area from inside the shirt to avoid flattening and taking away the puffiness. Since acrylic paint is permanent, the shirt can be put in the washer.

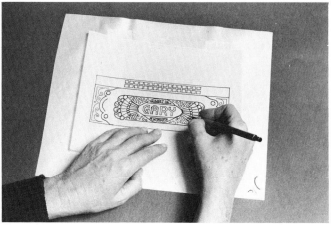

Trace and transfer design to fabric.

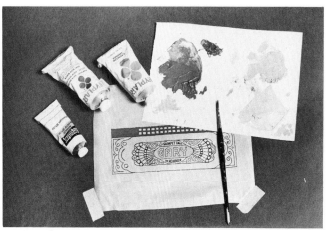

Paint different areas of appliqué.

Designs for appliqué.

Designer Stationery

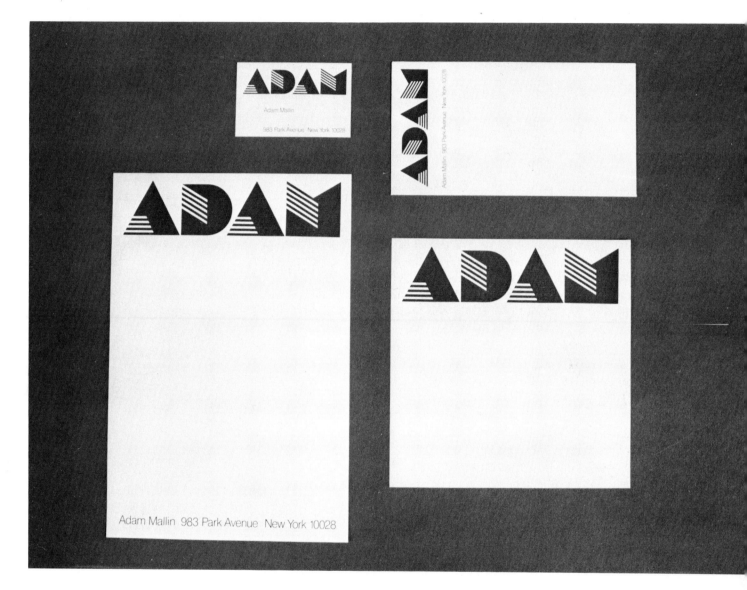

You can design your own stationery, prepare it for the printer, and have it professionally printed exactly the way you want it. The main advantage is that you can have unusual stationery on special paper for a fraction of the cost of buying it. Furthermore, if you want to make stationery to give as a gift and you don't have much time, this method is much faster than ordering it through a store.

The use of pressure-sensitive lettering, or "presstype," will enable you to design and prepare it easily. Presstype comes in sheets of transparent film. Hundreds of type styles and sizes are available

Use T-square and triangle to do the mechanical.

Rub presstype in position with end of pen.

from art supply stores and copy centers. You create a word by pressing one letter down at a time with a hard stylus or the end of a closed pen.

Select the typeface that suits your personality or mood. In addition you will need a T-square, drawing board or hard cutting surface, a triangle, rubber cement, a ruler, a hard pencil (3H), a fine, black ball-point pen, a 15 x 20-inch illustration board.

The stationery for Adam is printed in navy blue on gray paper. Adam had just turned thirteen and the design is straightforward and bold, reflecting his personality. Whether designing stationery for yourself or a friend, decide on the character you want to achieve. For instance, you may want a very sedate, elegant look; or perhaps a colorful, funky design; or, a businesslike feeling.

A presstype sample book will show how each typeface looks in different sizes. The sample books are on display in the art supply store where presstype is sold. Different typefaces appeal to different people, and you will no doubt be attracted to one that is best suited to you. Select the one that seems to achieve your look. It is similar to selecting clothing or furniture. The samples of various letterheads on these pages are to help you determine the style, size, and positioning of the type on your letterhead.

Begin by making a sketch of your name and address on plain paper and an envelope. This can be very rough in order to give you an idea of the size of presstype you want to use. Some people will prefer a small, subtle typeface. Once sketched, you can tell if you would rather have it larger. In this case you will select a larger typeface. Take your sketches to the art store when going to buy the presstype. The best-known companies that make presstype are Letraset, Presstype, Format, and Geotype.

The most popular sizes for stationery and envelopes are 8½ x 11 inches (typewriter paper size), which fits a no. 10 envelope that measures 4⅛ x 9½ inches, and Monarch size, which is 7¼ x 10½ inches with an envelope of 3⅞ x 7½ inches. The "Adam" stationery is Monarch size. It is commonly used for personal stationery.

Mark up presstype for photostating to size.

The presstype will be used to make up lines of type to be pasted up for the stationery and envelope. The directions for applying presstype are printed on the package and are quite simple to do. Take a plain piece of paper and draw a light pencil line to use as a guide for lining up the letters. Place the presstype in position and rub it down with the end of a marking pen. Keep the letters very close to one another, as this will give your stationery a more professional look. If your lines of type will fit on both the stationery and envelope, make them up for both uses; if not, have the type photostated to size for use on envelope, business cards, labels, etc. (See Friendship Frame project for photostat instructions.)

The type is pasted in position in the following way. In order to do the "pasteup" or "mechanical," you will need a drawing board or straight-edged table, a T-square, and a plastic triangle. Accuracy is extremely important, since the printer will reproduce whatever is on the pasteup. Tape the illustration board to your work surface. Draw a pencil outline of a rectangle that will be the size of your stationery and another outline for the envelope. Measure carefully. Using a ball-point pen, draw "cut lines" at each corner of the stationery. These are lines that will slightly extend the four sides of the rectangle. The printer will use these lines to indicate where to cut the paper and to get accurate placement. Cut lines are not necessary for the envelope. Next you will mount the presstype lines in position.

Cut your lines of type into strips for mounting. Lay a piece of tracing paper over the illustration board. Draw pencil lines on the tracing paper where the type is to be placed. Spread rubber cement on the back of the line of type. Lift the tracing paper overlay and place the type in position. Lower the tracing paper and make final adjustments by moving the type until it lines up exactly under the line on the tracing. Once you've mastered this technique you can prepare anything for printing. Make your own invitations, announcements, etc.

Take this pasteup to a printer. For fast, inexpensive printing I recommend the "Speedy," "Quick Copy," "One Day" variety of printer. They are listed in the Yellow Pages and are excellent for jobs that don't require special paper or very fine detail. For quality printing you will need a regular photo-offset printer who offers custom stationery printing. It will cost more and you should get an estimate before proceeding. They have a wide variety of paper stocks to choose from. At either type of printing shop you will want to decide on the quality, type of stock, color of the paper, and color of ink. Black ink on white paper costs the least. Colored stock is not much more than white, but special ink colors may cost considerably more than black.

The pressure-sensitive type used for the letterheads on the following pages is all from Letraset and the specifications are as follows: Annie Oakley is set in 60-point Playbill, running up the edge of the letterhead, ⅛-inch from the edge. Playbill is a typeface that is often seen on old posters and early American advertising. It has a bit of show business spirit.

Ken Randall is set in 60-point Lazybones, a well-named typeface. It is casual, almost like handwriting. This layout is casual as well. The letters don't line up in a formal way, but fit comfortably together. If this appeals to you, trace the letters on tracing paper and try various configurations until you get one that works for you. Then press the type down in position.

Bill Wilson is set in 36-point Microgramma Bold Extended. This is a semiformal typeface. Bill uses it for business, but the use of all lowercase letters in such a large size lets you know that is isn't a somber business.

Jill is set in 72-point Davida. She is a college student with a sense of humor. Jill picked Davida because it reminds her of the hats worn by jesters. Since she writes only to people who know her well, she felt that a last name was dispensable.

Margaret V. Ivers uses a monogram of initials set in 72-point Fritz Quadrata. The address line is set in 30-point Times New Roman. Her initials suggest a monogram that looks like roman numerals.

Like her friend Adam, Robin is set in Sinaloa and enlarged to fit the letterhead. The bold address line is set in Helvetica Medium and is printed in black on bright yellow paper. Subsequently it was reprinted in bright red on white.

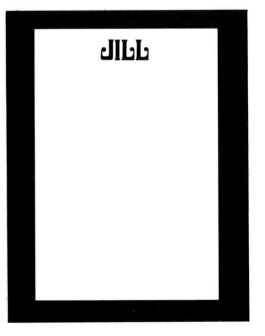

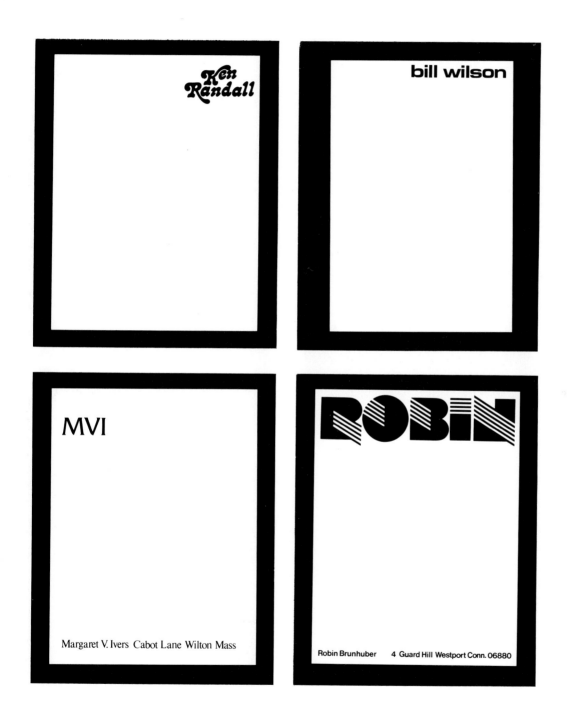

Ken Randall

bill wilson

MVI

Margaret V. Ivers Cabot Lane Wilton Mass

ROBIN

Robin Brunhuber   4 Guard Hill Westport Conn. 06880

Penny Lane is set in 72-point Cut-In Bold lowercase.

Karen Johnson is set in 48-point Avant-Garde Gothic Bold. The address line is set in 24-point Helvetica Extra Light. Avant-Garde is a typeface with many ligatures. That means that there are combinations of letters that are made into one unit. The K and A of Karen's name are joined as a ligature. This makes the name more distinctive.

Alan Volk is set in 36-point Souvenir Light. Alan's four-letter first and last names look well in this design. In order to make the idea work, words are abbreviated and hyphenated.

Barry Gordon uses bold initials set in 144-point Helvetica Medium lowercase. The address line is 24-point Helvetica Extra Light. Barry's nickname, "BG," serves as the basis for a graphic image.

Erica Nordstrom is a weaver. Her letterhead is set in 48-point Goudy Extra Bold. Used primarily for handwritten notes, this letterhead is cut short to fit the writer's needs.

Rebecca Watson uses a 72-point Serif Gothic overlapped slightly for her monogram. The address line is set in 24-point Windsor Elongated. Ms. Watson uses her monogram on the second sheets of her stationery and on her envelopes.

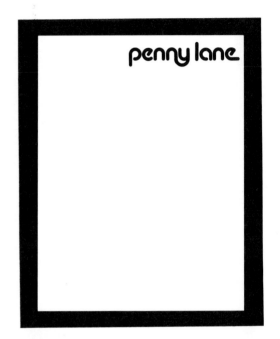

KAREN

Karen Johnson   236 West Riverview, Portland, Oregon

ALAN
VOLK
APT. 8
WILD-
WOOD
LANE
PHILA.
PENN.

erica nordstrom~weaver

14 magnolia lane raleigh   north carolina

Rebecca Watson 3 Cambrey Row Boston Massachusetts 20440

REW

People Pillows

The studio is big and bright and alive with creative energy. Collages and paintings of mixed media are scattered on the walls. Three-dimensional displays are in various stages of development. A soft sculpture of "The Fonz" lounges comfortably in a corner seat. He and pal J. J. Walker were commissioned works for a department store. Another creation for a magazine cover, a miniature wedding cake with the bride and groom sitting atop separate halves of a four-tiered vinyl cake in celebration of divorce, displays the humor often found in the work of its creator.

Jane de Jonge is an artist, sculptor, and designer with an impressive fine arts background. Her paintings, collages, and soft sculpture have appeared in numerous shows all over the country, many of which have earned her awards. She is a vibrant woman, constantly growing and aware of changing trends. Interested in developing new ideas, she is often involved with five things at once. While taking a sketch class, Jane met Joe Weishar. Heading his own company, New Visions, Mr. Weishar, a designer and consultant, is recognized for his creative work in the display field. Looking to develop new talents in this area, he encouraged Jane to expand her work into a wider market and is responsible for many of her commissions.

Together they formed a company called J & J and produced their first product, which was an instant hit with Bloomingdale's. *New York* magazine used it as one of their featured "Best Bets," and the following week J & J's six-foot silk-screened reclining Lady Sculpture bedrest pillow occupied a coveted place in Bloomingdale's New York window. A male companion, whom Jane affectionately refers to as a "manageable macho," immediately followed and the two were creatively christened "Imaginative Bedfellows."

The life-sized sculptures are sold as kits, ready to be decorated and stuffed. However, Jane has agreed to give us the instructions and pattern for making the marvelous lady from scratch. Designed as a six-foot-long replacement for headboard or bolsters, you can reduce the size so that the project can be used as a throw pillow, if you prefer. Jane has also included patterns for a small pillow to match. While the kits include a silk-screened front and back view of the lounging figure, yours can be drawn with fabric markers or acrylic paint. To personalize this project Jane suggests decorating the clothing with crewel, embroidery, lace, and appliqués. Add costume jewelry, a tattoo, or a name to her bikini. And you might let your imagination run wild over the rest of her.

Materials needed are: 100% cotton fabric (the amount to be determined according to the size of your project), zipper (36 inches

for a six-footer), scissors, ruler, polyester fiber filling or shredded polyurethane (a six-foot pillow takes eight to nine one-pound bags), decorative trim, a variety of acrylic paint, paint brush, black fabric marker (optional for drawing outline), tracing paper.

If you will be making a large pillow you will need several sheets of tracing paper in order to copy and scale your pattern up to size. This is best done a section at a time. Make a grid and copy the design, square for square, then transfer this to the fabric. You might consider using a roll of kraft paper to make the outline for the pattern to be used for cutting the large cloth pieces.

Once the design is transferred lightly in pencil, you can darken and make it permanent with a fabric marker or with acrylic paint. Once dry this paint is permanent on fabric and it can be washed in warm or cool water.

Begin by cutting out the six pattern pieces. With right sides together stitch one end of the long strip (A to F) to the matching top of the small triangular section, leaving a ⅝-inch seam allowance. Stitch the other end of the long strip (S to B) to the matching top of the large triangular section in the same way. Starting at corner H, stitch assembled pieces to pillow front, carefully matching points I, J, K, L, and M, ending at corner D. Clip into seam allowance at each of these points.

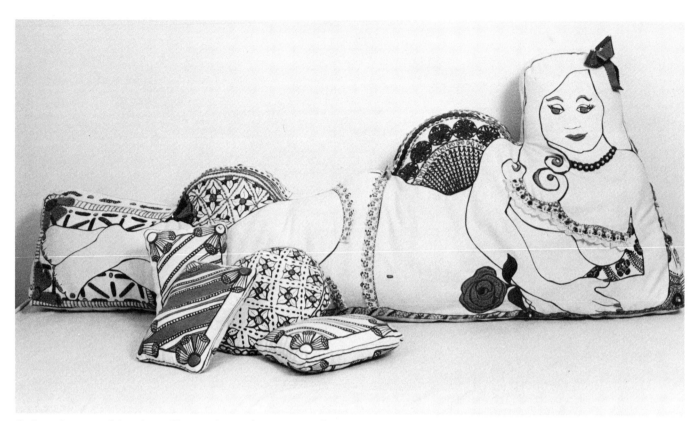

Soft sculpture is 6 feet long. Personalize with paint, needlepoint, embroidery, etc.

Measure an equal distance in from points C and G on both back and bottom sections, leaving a center space for the zipper. To make the six-foot pillow you will have 18 inches on both sides with a 36-inch opening for the zipper. Adjust these measurements according to the size of your pillow. Stitch the two sections together between G and the marked point, and C and the marked point. Fold back and press edges of the opening on the stitching line. Pin to the zipper tape along both sides and top stitch. Open the zipper partway and leave open. Stitch pillow back (with bottom now attached) to assembled pieces. To do this stitch along the top from corners G to C as you did for the front. Stitch the assembled pieces along the bottom from corners H to D.

Keep the pillow cover turned inside out and stitch together along seams H to G and D to C. Turn the pillow right side out through the zipper. It is now ready to stuff.

Fill the pillow with shredded polyurethane or polyester fiber filling or a combination of both. The soft sculpture is now ready for your personal touch. These directions are copyrighted by J & J and are included with each kit, along with painting suggestions. Another kit that Jane de Jonge and Joe Weishar make available provides the already sewn lady or man in black or white and ready for stuffing. See source of supplies for ordering information if you would like to eliminate the sewing in order to concentrate on the decoration. I imagine this could be a longtime needlecraft project. It might be a surefire attention stealer at the beach. For outdoor use Jane recommends heavy duty fabric, such as sailcloth or canvas.

124

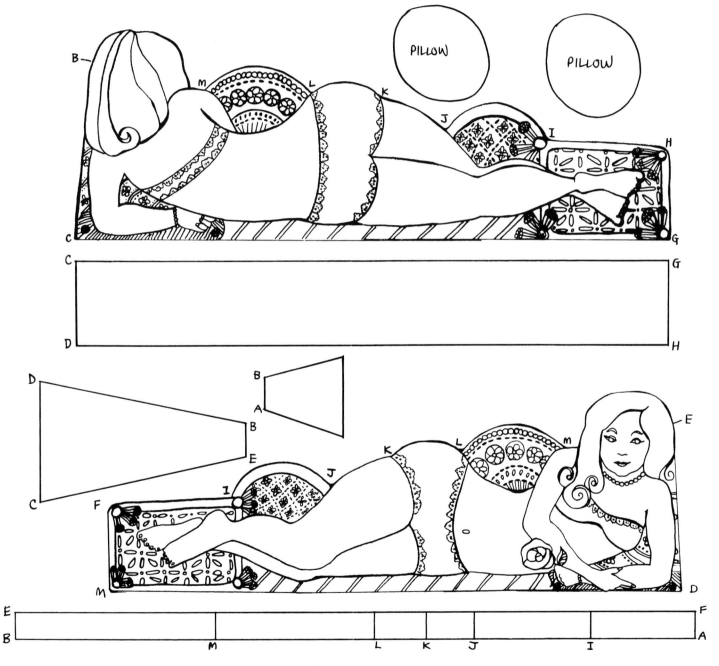

Boxes of cut pattern pieces lie in readiness at one end of the
studio, and Jane is anxious to explain the details for putting them
together. Her willingness to share her creation is a particularly appealing quality.

Plant Holder

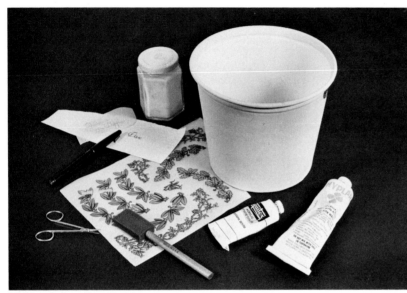

Materials for plant holder.

Write your message with permanent marker.

Visiting a friend in the hospital, going to a dinner party, or any occasion where a houseplant would be an appropriate gift, a plant holder need not be a problem. There are all varieties of plant pots to buy, but ours is personalized and costs practically nothing.

Paper paint pails are available wherever paint is sold and come in three different sizes. The cost is about thirty-five cents. They are sturdy even when wet, since they are used for mixing paint. The smooth white paper takes paint beautifully, or decorate one using the white background as is.

Materials needed are: paper paint bucket, paper cutouts, scissors, paint, brush, glue, varnish. Acrylic paint covers the surface in one application and goes on smoothly. Use an inexpensive sponge-type brush, which can be found in hardware and paint stores. The paint will dry quickly. Select designs that are easy to cut out and that will design well around the bucket. Wrapping paper is an excellent source for this project. I have made many of these pails in different sizes. Some have been decorated with large red poppies; others, a big sunflower. These were found easily on wrapping paper. For this project I used delicate leaves and berries, but you can also buy rub-on transfers in a craft shop. This will make it possible to avoid the delicate cutting required for a lacy design.

Once you have a design plan, decide where to put your message. Use black permanent marker to write on the painted pail. If it is a special occasion you can use the greeting paper to announce your message as part of the design. Birthday paper or a greeting

card has beautiful script letters, much nicer than what you can probably do freehand. Glue all paper down so that no edges are lifting up. Hold the bucket at arm's length and spray it with a coating of varnish. A high gloss finish is perfect. Three coats should be sufficient. Coat the inside as well for added protection.

If you enjoyed making this you might consider making more for other uses. I use them to hold mail, yarn, cosmetics, and knick-knacks in a child's room. They can be bright and colorful and decorated with any theme you choose. This is also a good project for a child to do because it is quick and easy and children like to see results immediately.

If children will be making this project, a few variations can make it easier for them. Magazines and coloring-book pictures are appealing to children and there is much to select from. A water-base polymer medium is substituted for the glue and varnish and is available in art supply and craft stores.

The polymer medium acts as a glueing agent as well as a varnish coating. It also prevents the picture from becoming transparent. Varnish will not work on magazine or coloring-book pictures. Coat the back of each cutout and press in place around the bucket. Brush a coating of the polymer medium over the whole thing. It dries in five minutes. If it gets on clothing, wash it off immediately. Once dry it is permanent. It is tough and will protect the paper designs and painted surface. Three or four applications are needed. Coat the inside of the bucket and rinse the brush clean in water.

Party Apron

This apron is pretty as well as practical. The eyelet, lace, and ribbon dress it up for party use and the quilted heart pocket is actually a removable pot holder. It is removed and reattached easily by adding a patch of Velcro to the apron and back of the pot holder. When not in use the pretty heart sits on your hip. When you go to grab something hot, you don't have to wonder where you put the pot holder. The heart is made with a quilted painting technique and the pattern is shown actual size. The apron is a simple grocer's style that you can make in no time. Add the decorative trim of your choice. Fabric and notions stores have a tremendous variety of lace and ribbon as well as buttons and sequins. I used the kind of eyelet that you weave a ½-inch ribbon through. The red satin ribbon matches the heart and is especially nice against the white background.

The materials needed are: ⅞-yard white broadcloth, canvas or cotton of 45 inches (or more) wide, 2½ yards of ½-inch wide satin ribbon, 2 yards of lace trim, 1¼ yards of eyelet, 2-ounce tube of red acrylic paint, paint brush, cotton batting, scissors, small package of Velcro.

Using the apron pattern provided, scale up to measure 12 inches across the top. Cut out one piece for the apron. Press under all edges of the apron ¼-inch. Press under again ¼-inch on all edges and stitch.

Cut a piece of lace slightly longer than the width of the apron hem. Pin this under the hem, folding back raw edges at the sides and stitch across. Cut two strips of lace for the top and pin in place, leaving room for the eyelet and ribbon to be stitched over the top raw edge of the lace. Stitch the lace to the apron, folding the raw side edges to the inside of the apron.

Cut a length of eyelet ribbon to fit across the top and bottom of the apron, leaving enough to fold inside on each end. Cut two pieces of ½-inch red satin ribbon the same length as the eyelet. Weave the ribbon through each piece of eyelet and stitch to the top and bottom of the apron.

Cut ribbon lengths for ties at the waist and around the neck. Stitch the ends of the ribbon in place, using a cross stitch.

Party apron pattern.

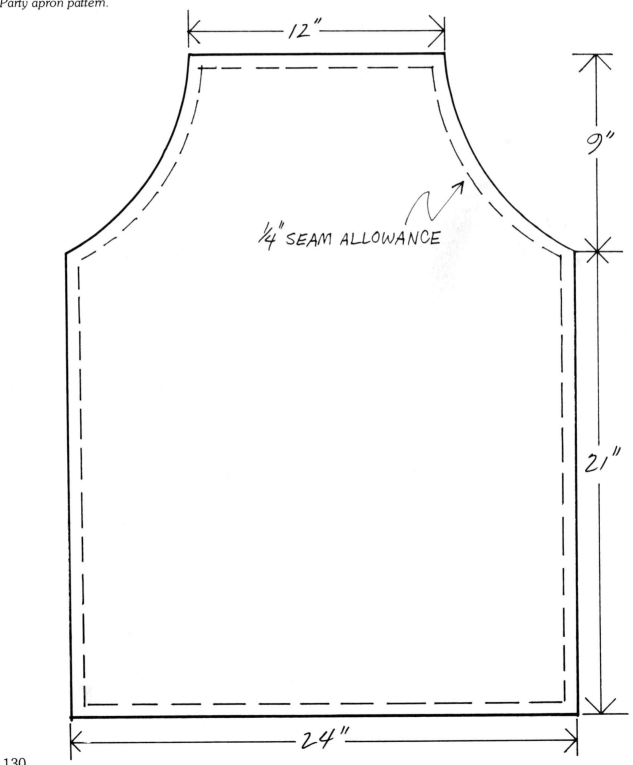

12"

¼" SEAM ALLOWANCE

9"

21"

24"

Heart Pot Holder

Use the same material for the pot holder. Trace the heart pattern shown exactly as is. Use a small flat square bristle brush to fill in the paint. Every other heart outline is painted with acrylic paint. Grumbacher or cadmium red are bright colors and excellent for this. Since so little paint is needed for this, you can buy the smallest, or 2-ounce tube, available. The paint is of a fairly thick consistency and can be thinned with a little water, or, if you want a lighter shade of red, white paint will cut the color. Be careful not to thin the paint too much, as it will bleed when applied to the fabric. Make a test on a patch of the fabric before beginning.

Trace an initial from page 61 for the center of the smallest heart and paint it with a small, pointed artist's brush. When the entire heart has been painted and is dry, cut around it, leaving an extra edge of ¼ inch. Cut another piece of fabric exactly to this size for the back. Cut a piece of cotton batting (sold in fabric stores) the exact size of the heart. This will not meet at the edges of the fabric. Set this piece aside.

With right sides together pin the two hearts together and stitch around the edges, leaving a ¼-inch seam. You will be stitching around the actual heart outline. Leave a 2-inch opening so that you can turn the heart inside out. Trim seams and clip around curved edges before turning.

Slip the heart-shaped batting material inside and flatten it out so that it fits properly. Slip stitch the opening. Stitch around each

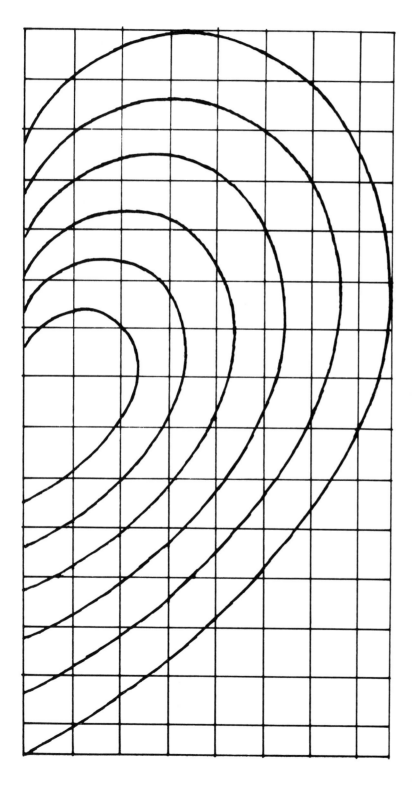

Pot holder is easily removed.

132

Pot holder is reattached to Velcro spot.

outline of the painted heart, creating a quilted effect.

Velcro can be found in a small package in any notions store. There are two parts. Sew one half on the back of the pot holder. Decide where you want to place it on the apron. Adjust the angle and sew the other piece of Velcro onto the apron. The heart pot holder can be fastened securely and removed easily, again and again. The apron and the heart can be washed as you would normally. Acrylic paint is permanent on any fabric.

If you don't want to bother making an apron, you might consider using the painted quilt technique in different patterns on several pot holders. A geometric design, for instance, would work well. Keep it simple, as this technique looks best when the design is bold and the painting doesn't have to be too intricate. If you enjoy working with miniatures for doll houses, this might be a very cute way to make a tiny quilt for an old-fashioned bed. And for really ambitious people, how about a wall hanging!

Needlepoint College Pillow

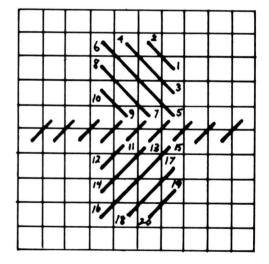

Will it be finished by graduation?

Robin, whose older sister, Lisa, is a student at the University of Connecticut, wanted to design a needlepoint pillow using the UConn logo and the entering and graduating dates. First she planned the design on graph paper to determine the size of the pillow, letters, and stitches to be used. Lisa's dormitory room is brown and yellow. Robby decided to use these colors with red for the numbers, yellow for UCONN, and brown for the background. She colored in the paper design to see how the colors would look together. She then counted and measured out each letter so that it would be properly centered and spaced, and outlined it with a colored pencil. Of course, since each school name is different, this project is more a suggestion for an idea than a design to follow.

Each background square of sixteen holes is worked with a Scotch stitch that is reversed on every other square. This is done in dark brown. The lines between each square were done with a Continental stitch in a lighter brown. The letters are done the same way with a Scotch stitch in yellow, separated by white Continental stitch lines.

Halfway through this project Robby started her midterm exams. The needlepoint was quickly forgotten and it took a lot of effort for her to finish. For a while, everyone thought that Lisa would surely graduate before the pillow was completed. Fortunately the pillow is not large. It measures 8½ x 11 inches. Robby finished it off and made it into a pillow, using brown corduroy for the back.

135

Formal Photographs

Weddings, graduation, proms, holiday formals, and anniversaries are always reasons for taking pictures. A lace background seems appropriate for such photographs. However, when I tried to find lace in fabric stores, I was told that they didn't carry it. I then went to a notions store that just happened to have some very old, antique lace that was very expensive. I decided that if it was this difficult to find the materials then a substitute was required, or I would have to forget this project. Paper doilies are perfect. They are lacy and come in a variety of sizes. Best of all, they are inexpensive and easy to find. Almost all card shops and five-and-ten-cent stores carry a wide variety, and, if you prefer, silver or gold can be used rather than the traditional white.

For this project I wanted to use three separate photos in one frame. The size of your photograph and the number to be used will

Cut mat board for photos.

determine the size of your frame. These photos are 3 x 5-inch and are trimmed to fit a 9 x 12-inch frame. Because there are three, I wanted to crop them so that there would be plenty of room for a border of lace.

The materials needed are: a T-square and triangle (a must), regular color snapshots 3 x 5-inch, X-acto knife, illustration board (available in art stores), 3H pencil, package of doilies, mat polymer medium (art or craft store), inexpensive 1-inch sponge brush, 1¼ yards of lace trim or ribbon, 9 x 12-inch frame.

Lightly draw a rectangle 9 x 12 inches on the illustration board, using your 3H pencil. Within this rectangle you will draw smaller rectangles to fit your photographs. Measure and plan this before making your outlines. With a metal straightedge and very sharp X-acto knife, cut out the rectangles. It is best to make four light strokes over and over rather than one hard cut. Press down with your knife blade on the board and resting right against your straightedge. This will insure a precise, clean line. Since the separation between the photographs is so thin, be careful not to cut through them by accident. This work requires a certain amount of precision, so take your time. If the cut lines are crooked the finished project will look sloppy and unprofessional.

Lay the doilies on the mat so that they overlap. Arrange and rearrange them until they cover the entire background area. There should be enough to overlap on the edges and to fold inside the cutout sections in the center. To attach this to the illustration board

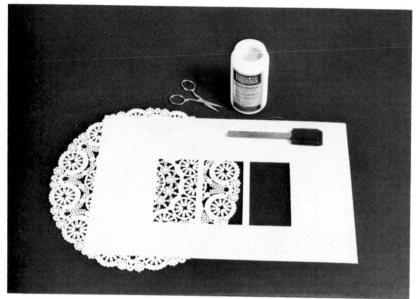

Materials for lace-covered background.

Medium used as glue and overcoating.

you will use mat polymer medium. This is a milky white liquid that looks like Elmer's glue. It is used as a gluing agent as well as a protective coating like varnish. It is available in craft shops and art supply stores and comes in a glossy or mat finish. The mat is best for this project because it will make the doily look more like real lace. The medium dries within ten minutes and has a water base, so it can be washed off hands, table surface, and clothes. However,

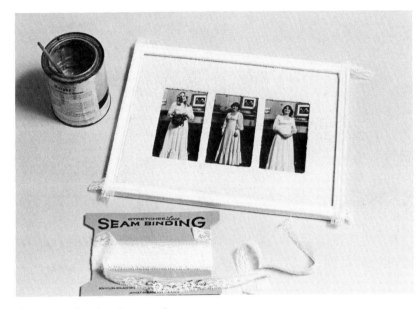

Lace trim finishes frame edges.

it should be cleaned up before it dries. The sponge-type brush used to apply this is found in all hardware stores and often used for touch-up paint jobs.

Spread the medium over a small section at a time, as it dries quickly. Place the doily over the area and spread the medium on top of the doily. This will dry clear. Keep adding more doily pieces in this way until the background is covered. Make diagonal cuts at the corners of the inside rectangles and fold the doily back. Apply some of the medium to the back of the board to secure the doily pieces. Coat the entire lace-covered background.

Tape the photographs in position from the back and place the entire thing in the frame. To finish off overall lacy effect, I added a trim of lace ribbon to the edge of the frame. Cover the frame with the medium and run the trim around the frame. Clip off any excess at the corners. For an added touch I coated the trim with an oil-base wood varnish which yellowed it slightly so that it looks antiqued. This is not at all necessary, unless you have the varnish and would like to try this technique. If you choose to use the varnish, you can use the same brush, but since the varnish has an oil base the brush must be cleaned in mineral spirits or thrown away when finished. The varnish is also long-drying and the project should be put aside overnight.

The girls in the photograph are sisters and gave this as a gift to their parents for Christmas. It's a pretty way to preserve a memorable event. They are each wearing their prom dresses.

Batik Shirts

Batik, a Javanese word for wax painting, is the application of wax to certain areas of material which is then dyed. The wax is applied hot so that it flows easily and penetrates the material. The wax portions are protected and will not absorb the dyes. As a result a pattern or design appears in these areas once the wax is removed.

While little is known of the origin of batik, many think the technique originated in China. Others believe it to be an outgrowth of India's method for decorating clothes that dates back twelve hundred years. The fabrics used were confined to cotton and silks, which is primarily what we use today. The dyes used by the natives were originally vegetable. The range of colors was not very great, however, and the natives who practiced the art of batik were more concerned with the intricacy of design than the delicacy of color. It was not until the latter part of the nineteenth century that the great strides made in the production of dyes led artists to experiment with them as a medium and to the revival of the two thousand-year-old art. The first of these artists were from Holland, and, equipped with an almost unlimited range of color produced by modern dyes, they created designs that were never before realized.

Modern techniques vary only slightly from those employed originally, the main difference being in the improved equipment. You don't need expensive or complicated tools to create a simply designed piece of clothing. Once you have learned the technique, using one color sufficiently, you will be able to do more elaborate batik designs, perhaps employing the use of several colors.

A pot is simmering on the stove and sputtering sounds burst from a hot-plate burner on the counter. The sink is filled with dark blue liquid and it is obvious that no cooking is taking place. "I'd like to get out of the kitchen once in awhile . . . maybe for good," said Karen Kalkstein, looking not at all like a harried housewife. Her kitchen surroundings are a necessary part of Karen's craft, although she's looking forward to moving everything into the studio that she and her husband, Sean, are adding to their home.

A room off the kitchen has been turned into a work area as well, although Karen seems at home wherever she can spread her work out. Karen Kalkstein designs original batik T-shirts which are personalized for friends, her two children—Jed and Kendall—a handful of exclusive boutiques, and for magazine mail-order offers.

Karen has grown up with crafts ever present in her background, thus developing an ability to work on many levels. Known for years as a painter, then as a potter, she admits to having a greater passion for craftwork than painting. Having taken a variety of craft classes, she finds that a career as a professional craftworker affords a peace-

Fill in design areas with hot wax.

ful existence. The involvement in many crafts has developed Karen's keen sense of design. "Some of the shirts display simple coloring book shapes, others are my creations, like this unicorn," she says, while pulling out the shirt from a stack of various sizes and colors. Karen says that crafting is relaxing. Once the technique is perfected, your mind is free to develop new ideas as you work. This stimulating aspect is different from that felt when she is painting, which requires more concentration. Batik, in particular, inspires a kind of unrestrained freedom, encouraging experimentation; a necessity to growth. Karen enjoys this aspect of crafting and makes the most of it.

To make a T-shirt batik you will need: an all-cotton white T-shirt, batik dye (such as Fibrec or Dylon, available in craft shops), a pot large enough to hold the shirt, salt, fixative (if not included in the dye), canning wax (available in hardware stores or supermarkets), pencil, newspaper, large, stiff bristle paint brush, rubber gloves, full apron, a can for melting the wax.

To begin, decide what kind of design you would like to create. If this will be a project for a child, choose a simple design, such as those found in coloring books. Karen says that it is easiest to trace and wax big blocks of a picture. If you use the designs provided here you can trace right from the book. Place the T-shirt over the area and trace lightly with a pencil. If you want to enlarge or reduce a picture, first trace, then transfer the outline to the shirt.

The canning wax or paraffin comes in a package of several blocks and is quite inexpensive. Place one of the chunks in an empty can which is then set in a shallow pan of barely boiling water. The wax will melt and should not be left too long. It is best if used before it gets too thin. Always heat wax in a can set in water, as it sputters and can cause a fire if the can is set right on the burner. Karen uses a hot plate with an old pan filled with wax. In this way she can control the heat.

Fold sheets of newspaper to form padding to slide inside the shirt. Dip your paint brush into the hot wax and paint around the outline that you've drawn. Lines that butt each other should not be

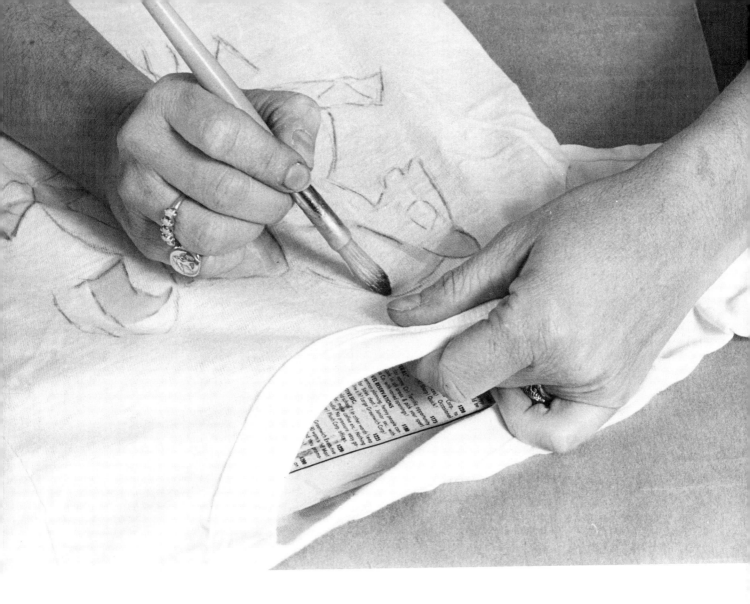

waxed at one time. Wax large areas of the design that will remain white. Leave spaces between where you want the color to take. Check from time to time to be sure that the shirt is not sticking to the paper inside. If the wax isn't hot enough it won't seep through the shirt as completely as necessary. Reheat when needed. In order to get an idea of how your finished work will look, hold the shirt up to the light or check the back of the design as you go along. As each area is waxed, let it cool before going on to the next. When all areas of the design are waxed it is time to prepare the dye bath.

Begin by donning rubber gloves and a full apron. Since the dye you use should be permanent, be sure the apron is one you don't care about. Since we will be using only one color choose one that you like best for the background. The areas that have been waxed will remain white. Dye colors look very intense in the package, but usually create a pastel color on the shirt.

The directions for the dye process are given on each package. However, Karen uses the following method for her dyeing: Fill the sink with cold water. Empty the contents of the package into one cup of warm water and stir until it is completely dissolved. Add the dissolved dye to the sink water and stir until mixed. Now add the

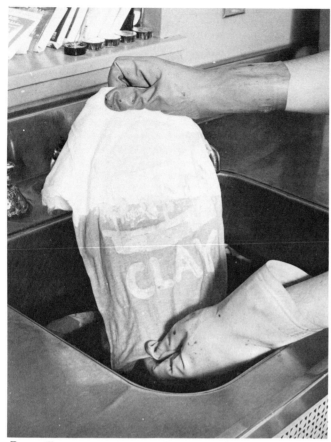

Dye will not penetrate waxed areas.

Rinse in boiling water to remove wax.

T-shirt and stir slowly for 10 minutes. Add three ¼ cups of salt at 5-minute intervals, stirring continuously. The dye that she uses contains the fixative which must be dissolved in one cup of hot tap water. Add this to the dye bath and stir slowly for 10 minutes. Keep the shirt submerged for 30 minutes, stirring occasionally. Check the color for intensity. If it isn't dark enough, leave it sitting for a while longer.

Bring a pot of soapy water to a boil. Karen prefers Ivory Flakes. Dip the shirt into the boiling water to melt out the wax. Rinse again to be sure all wax residue is dissolved. Then rinse in cold water and hang up to dry. When the shirt is dry, iron and wear it.

Karen's children have designed their own T-shirts, using their own made-up drawings. This might be a project your children would like to do with you, because it definitely needs supervision. When craftwork is a part of your everyday life, it often dictates the style in which you live. The Kalksteins and their children enjoy an easygoing routine which allows for spontaneity. It was Friday afternoon and the children were home from school early. A light snow began to fall as they rummaged around for their ski gear. Since both parents work at home, they take advantage of the freedom this affords. "What about the 104 T-shirt orders that must be delivered next week?" I naively asked. "Simple," Karen said, "I just pack up my wax, shirts, and burner with everything else. There's always sitting time and I'll dye them all at once when I get home on Sunday." Sure enough, by Wednesday I received the unicorn shirt I had ordered.

Samantha Rochlin models her batik shirt.

Xerox Transfer

You can create your own artwork to be made into a clothing transfer. It might be a child's painting from school or a graphic design that you've drawn. If you have a business or personal message that you want to advertise it is not at all difficult or expensive to do. If you aren't an artist, but want a pretty design that you create, trace one from a book or similar source. The graphic art-books and magazines in the library might give you ideas. Children's books and coloring books are good sources of large, simple graphic symbols for original art. If you know someone who is starting a business you could design a logo for fun and give the shirt as a

Draw design backwards.

Use bright colors and contrast.

celebration gift. They can be humorous, delicate, elaborate, bold, anything you can think of.

Bob Quinn is a college student. He paints houses in the summer and feels that he does a better job than many of his competitors. We thought it would be an added touch of professionalism if he wore a personalized shirt when going to give estimates. Once the original drawing is complete it is just as easy to have several transfers made from it, and the cost is slightly over one dollar apiece. So Bob thought it would be appropriate for his co-workers to have "Quinn for Quality Paint Co." shirts as well.

The art is transferred to a wax backing. This is done on a special Xerox machine, offered at most copy centers. Check your local Yellow Pages to locate a place.

The materials needed are few: tracing paper, black marker, selection of brightly colored markers, a piece of silver foil, an iron, and a piece of clothing (white is usually best and cotton works well).

Begin by finding or creating the design of your choice. Trace it either same size or scale to desired size, but no larger than 8½ x 14 inches. The design must then be retraced so that it is backwards, especially where letters are concerned. Your design will read correctly when transferred to the shirt.

The original design and two copies.

Outline the design with black marker so that it is readable and fill in with desired color. The colors will darken when transferred, so keep this in mind when choosing colors to be used. The brighter the better. Also, it is best not to use two dark or two light colors next to each other. Be sure to have contrast. Take your tracing paper art to the copy center and they will make as many transfers as you want. They can do it while you wait, as this takes only minutes.

To fuse the transfer to clothing, place the shirt on your ironing board. Center the transfer facedown and place a piece of silver foil over the back. Set your iron at medium hot and apply pressure to the foil-covered transfer. This will prevent scorching of the paper. Test to see if the art is transferring by peeling back a corner of the paper. If it isn't, your iron isn't hot enough. When properly heated and enough pressure is applied the paper backing will peel away easily, leaving a printed shirt. The clothing can be washed in warm or cool water, but do not place it in a hot dryer. Iron from the wrong side.

148

Collector's Tote Bag

This is a collector's tote bag. It is decorated with memorabilia held in stitched plastic pockets on the front. My mother, Ruth Linsley, lives in Florida and collected the shells, seaweed, and beach flowers while beachcombing. Your bag might display pressed flowers, snapshots, or other collectibles that have meaning to you.

Materials needed are: a ½-yard of heavy fabric, such as canvas, duckcloth, etc., a piece of 8 x 11-inch clear plastic, 40 inches of webbing tape for straps, 2 feet of lace trim (optional), 2 snaps, ruler, pins, pencil.

Measure and draw rectangles for the pattern pieces on the fabric. Cut out. Hem the pockets ½-inch all around. Turn the top edge of the back of the bag under from the wrong side to right side ½-

inch. Turn again 2 inches. Press and stitch down. Fold outside back pocket down 1½ inches from top and up 5¾ inches from the bottom. Place the pocket in the outside center of the back 1-inch below the turned hem. Sew across the flap and around the sides and bottom.

Next place the smaller pocket on the inside front 3½ inches from the top center and sew in place. This can be used for eyeglasses, pencils, suntan lotion, etc.

Fold ½-inch of the top front down from the wrong side to the right. Turn down another 2 inches and pin on the sides in order to hold firmly. Fold the bottom edge up 2 inches and pin on the sides to hold.

Cut the plastic material 8 x 11 inches and center it on the bag front. Slip this under the top hem about a ½-inch. Place memorabilia in a pleasing composition under the plastic. Slip the bottom of the plastic under the bottom hem.

Run the lace trim along the sides of the plastic, slipping it under the top and bottom hems. Sew around each picture and down the sides and across the hems at the top and bottom.

Place tape handles 3 inches from the side edges with the ends inside and sew across the top. Turn ½-inch of the sides of the bag inside and sew around three sides. If you make this tote bag of a neutral color you'll be able to wear it with everything. This is a great size for a beach bag, marketing tote for small items, or a school bag for the kids. For children, you might display pictures of things that are particularly appealing to them. Adjust the memorabilia to the individual taste of the person who will receive it.

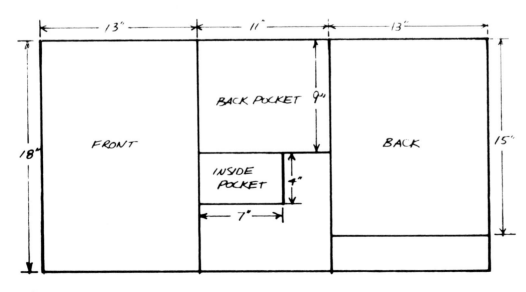

Monogrammed Clutch Purse

A good-looking, quick project that can be completed in less than an hour is this suede clutch purse. It is made in a rich, creamy tan color that goes with almost everything, and the fabric has some terrific qualities. It cuts like butter and doesn't need any hemming. It is soft and takes a painted stencil monogram beautifully.

First draw a rectangle that when folded in half becomes the opened up size of the bag. The actual clutch size will be half again when finished and the bag is folded for use. The finished bag measures 11 x 15 inches.

Finish each end by spraying one inch of the back, top, and bottom edges with Spra-Ment fabric adhesive. Turn the edges down. Thus, no stitches are needed, which would not look well on the front of the bag. Fold the fabric so that the right sides are together and stitch up both sides, leaving a ¼-inch seam. Turn your bag right side out and fold in half for a comfortable carrying size.

To add a monogram I used white acrylic paint, a sheet of stencil letters, and a stipple brush. An artist's brush is fine, if you work carefully, applying paint from edges toward the center. Decide how and where your initials should be arranged and placed.

Using a small amount of paint, hold the stipple brush vertically and tap up and down repeatedly until the stencil area is filled in with color. Do not overload your brush when reapplying the paint. Keep tapping over and over until the area is completely coated and the fabric no longer bleeds through.

For added protection, the outside of the clutch can be given a quick overall spray with Scotchgard fabric protector. That's it, and you can use it as soon as the paint or spray dries.

PLUS JE BOIS
MIEUX JE CHANTE!

CHAMPAGNE
Pre MARQUE

CURAÇAO
COGNAC
RHUM

Designer Greeting Cards

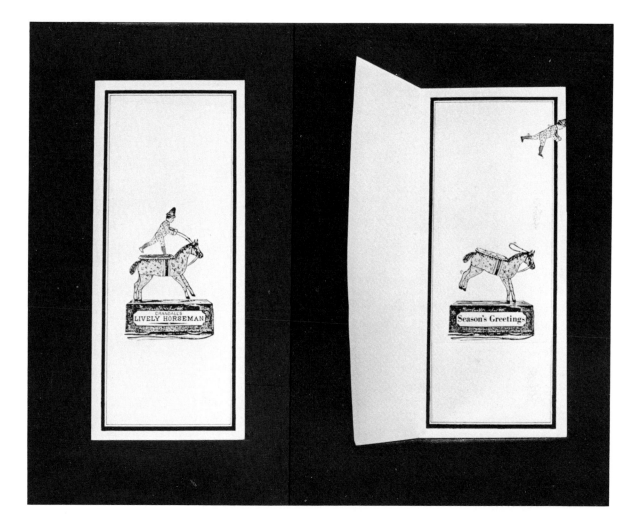

This Christmas we received a holiday greeting card from Mike Aron, a design student at Cooper Union. It was so clever that it seemed like a good project to include as an example of how you can design your own greeting cards, announcements, invitations, place cards, etc.

If you need only a few dozen copies of a greeting card, Xerox copies offer interesting possibilities. Mike's was made from an old engraving. Two copies of the man on the horse were made and pasted in position in the border. Then many copies were made of the pasteup. The copies were then cut out and mounted on the front and inside of the card. They were then colored by hand. This card reflects Michael Aron's particular sense of humor and is therefore more personal than anything he could have bought. Use the art from the preceding page to design your own cards.

Address Oval

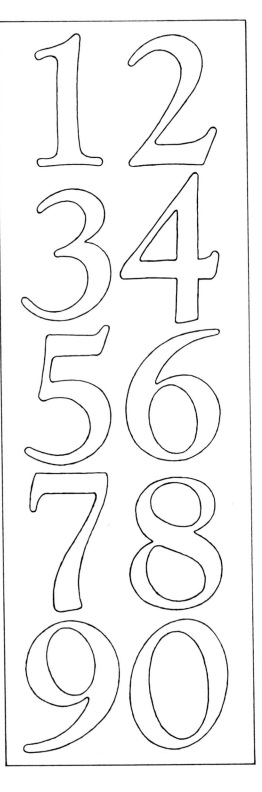

An address plaque is a wonderful personalized house-warming gift. You can use either a name or number for the design. The decoration is done with the technique of decoupage. This oval is made of 1-inch pine and can be placed on the front door of a house or apartment. This oval is not a standard craft shop item, but you can have the shape cut at a lumberyard. If you have a saber or coping saw it is quite simple to cut one yourself.

The materials needed are: tracing paper, wooden oval plaque, white paint, ½ to 1-inch paint brush, black permanent marker, one small piece each of medium and fine grit sandpaper, cuticle scissors, paper illustrations to cut out, white glue, sponge, small can of polyurethane varnish, brush cleaner, brass screw-type ring for hanging.

Trace the oval shape to use as a pattern guide for cutting it yourself or for the lumberyard. Using the medium grit sandpaper, sand all edges and front and back until smooth. Next paint all exposed areas. Acrylic paint covers well and dries quickly. However, if you have regular house paint on hand, use it. When dry, sand lightly and recoat if necessary. Sand again.

Trace and transfer the numbers to the plaque. Center or place them to one side, depending on how many you use and the relationship to the designs selected. Fill in the outline with black permanent marker.

The illustrations you will need can be found in books, greeting cards, wrapping paper, postcards, wallpaper, and similar sources. Avoid magazine pictures as the paper is too thin and not good for

this project. Cut the designs out with sharp cuticle scissors. Try to cut as close to the outline as possible, eliminating all excess paper. Arrange the designs around the numbers until you have a final layout. Attach each cutout to the oval with white glue, such as Elmer's. Pat away excess glue with a damp sponge.

Coat the front and sides with polyurethane varnish. This will begin to create a hard, tough finish that will protect the oval even outdoors. Let this dry overnight and continue to apply layer upon layer of varnish, letting each dry before the next is applied. After three or four coats, sand the surface lightly, using the fine sandpaper. Five to ten coats should be sufficient. The back will require two or three coats of varnish as well.

Screw the brass ring into the center of the top for hanging. Finish off the oval with a coat of furniture paste wax for an added protective covering. Buff until a shiny finish is achieved.

Garden Basket

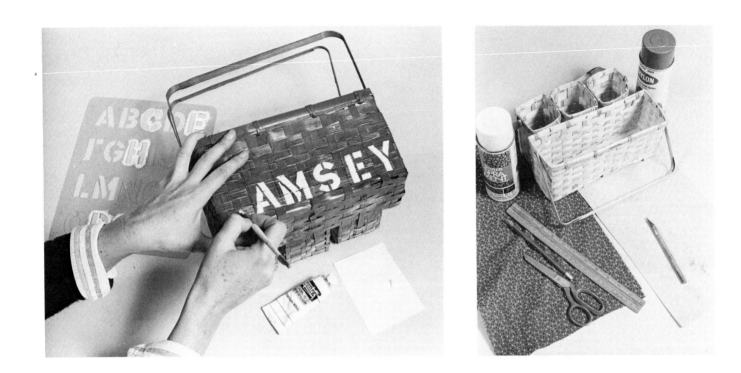

With so many home gardeners tending indoor plants, a garden basket to hold small tools, clippers, and a misting bottle can be decorated and filled for gift giving. This basket is the inexpensive kind, used as a picnic condiments carrier. Most places that sell baskets carry them. While crudely made, a quick coating with spray paint gives it a colorful, shiny finish. The design is painted over this and calico fabric lining gives the basket a pretty, country look.

Materials needed are: a small can of green enamel spray paint, pen or marker, sheet of stencil letters, small tubes of white, yellow, and blue acrylic paint, ½-yard of calico cotton fabric, Spra-Ment fabric adhesive, pointed artist's brush.

Give the basket a coating of spray paint and let dry thoroughly. Using the stencil sheet, outline the letters of the name with pen or marker. Leave a space between the letters to draw the stems of the tulips. Draw the tulips and leaves. It is not a smooth surface, so the design should be kept simple and easy so that you can draw freehand. Fill in the outlined letters with white acrylic paint. Paint the tulips and leaves. Let this dry.

156

Next measure and cut sections of the fabric to use as a liner for each section of the basket. Each piece should be slightly larger than the area to be covered, in order to fold under raw edges. Spray the back of the fabric pieces with Spra-Ment adhesive. Fold down all top edges and press the fabric down so that it sticks to itself. Respray this top area of the hem so that all inside fabric is sticky. Place the bottom pieces inside the basket first. Next line the walls and press the fabric against the inside of the basket with the palm of your hand while pressing from the outside with the other. The adhesive will allow the fabric to stick securely to the basket. No sewing is necessary.

For an added touch you might like to spray the handles of the wooden tools. These usually come unfinished and the raw wood takes the spray paint well. Fill the basket with seed packets, garden gloves, etc.

Embroidery Designs

Embroidery is a beautiful way to paint with stitches. To personalize a blouse or a pocket on a skirt with a floral initial often turns an ordinary gift into something special. However, it is often difficult to find delicate designs that lend themselves to this craft. An embroidered initial could be added to a napkin for a table setting, the hem of a pillowcase, the top edge of the tote bag, a solid heart pocket, a silk scarf, a handkerchief. You might even turn one into a personalized appliqué. I thought you might enjoy adapting some of these initials for other crafting projects as well. Outline and paint one on the front of a greeting card or scale it down for a scrimshaw pendant, or scale it up for a batik design.

Combine initial with design.

ABCDEFG

HIJKLMN

OPQRSTU

VWXYZ

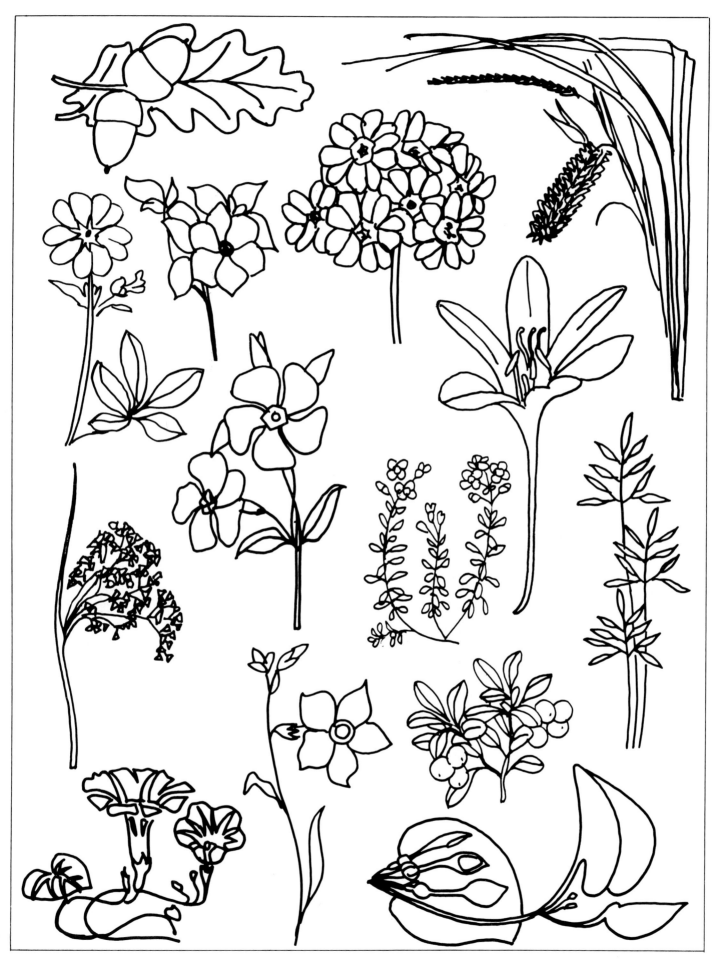

It's the Process That Counts

Over the years I have known many artists and craftworkers. We all seem to have one obvious thing in common. Crafts are a very integral part of one's everyday life and most crafters seem to work anywhere in the house, often everywhere. It starts out slowly, taking up perhaps only cupboard space, if the craft isn't as imposing as stained glass. Little by little it creeps into the bedroom, kitchen, wherever the person feels most comfortable. Rarely do we have the luxury of a separate studio. One crafter converted an unused bedroom into a working studio. It was probably the neatest and most unused room in the house. "I start up there in the morning," she confided, "but by ten I'm ready for coffee, and while I'm in the kitchen I may do more work. The phone rings and it's a good opportunity to pick up my work while chatting." Others feel that they want to work while being with the family in the evening or find that a bedroom has the best light at certain times of the day.

Since most crafters work alone they don't often have the opportunity to hear from other creative people unless an effort is made to form such a group. It is therefore fulfilling for me to know that I am contributing to the line of communication between craftworkers all over the country. In this way we are able to share design ideas, personal techniques, and individual work habits.

I am often talking to crafters in their homes where they work. It is obvious that *every* member of the craftworker's family is usually aware of the creative process that moves in and makes itself quite at home. This is an unconscious contribution that we give our spouses, children, and friends who come to visit. If you feel that you should be sweeping the evidences of your crafting under the carpet to make way for others, it might be comforting to know that the state of being in "the process of" is often more important than the finished project.

Sources of Supplies

All the supplies and tools used to make the various projects can be found in local craft and art supply stores. However, if you can't find something, the following list of suppliers have a mail-order service and most will send a catalog on request.

Art Supplies
Arthur Brown, Inc.
2 West 46th St.
New York, N.Y. 10036

Baskets
Boycan's Craft Supplies
Mail Order Division
P.O. Box 897
Sharon, Penn. 16146

Fran's Basket House
89 W. Main St.
Rockaway, N.J. 07866

Batik materials
Aljo Mfg. Co.
116 Prince St.
New York, N.Y. 10012

Fibrec Inc.
2815 18th St.
San Francisco, Calif. 94107

Naturalcraft
2199 Bancroft Way
Berkeley, Calif. 94704

Calico for appliqué
The Weston Country Store
Weston, Vt. 05161

Decoupage supplies
American Handicrafts Co.
P.O. Box 2911
Fort Worth, Tex. 76101

Connoisseur Studio, Inc.
Box 7187
Louisville, Ky. 40207

Hazel Pearson
4128 Temple City Blvd.
Rosemead, Calif. 91770

The O-P Craft Co.
425 Warren St.
Sandusky, Ohio 44870

Embroidery materials
Lee Wards Creative Crafts Ctr.
12 Saint Charles St.
Elgin, Ill. 60120

Merribee Needlecraft Co.
2904 West Lancaster
Fort Worth, Tex. 76107

The Needlewoman Shop
146 Regent St.
London, WIR 6 BA England

Fabric for heart pockets and holiday gift bag
Fabrications
146 East 56th St.
New York, N.Y. 10022

General craft supplies
American Handicrafts Co.
P.O. Box 2911
Fort Worth, Tex. 76101

Boycan's Craft Supplies
Mail Order Division
P.O. Box 897
Sharon, Penn. 16146

Hazel Pearson Handicrafts
4128 Temple City Blvd.
Rosemead, Calif. 91770

J. L. Hammett Co.
Hammett Place
Braintree, Mass. 02184

Herbs for potpourri
Caswell-Massey Co. Ltd.
518 Lexington Ave.
New York, N.Y. 10017

Miss Plum's Particulars
66 Church La.
Westport, Conn. 06880

Wide World of Herbs Ltd.
11 Catherine St. East
Montreal, 129 P. Quebec,
   Canada

Needlepoint supplies for projects listed
The Hartsdale Home Center
208 E. Hartsdale Ave.
Hartsdale, N.Y. 10530

Plexiglas
Mail Order Plastics
56 Lispenard St.
New York, N.Y. 10013

Plastic Center Inc.
1215–1221 Wood St.
Philadelphia, Penn. 19107

Scrimshaw supplies
Donald R. Kostecki
Lapidary Supplies
6245 No. Fairfield
Chicago, Ill. 60659

P. J. McNally
144 Chambers St.
New York, N.Y. 10007

Stencil supplies
Stencil Magic
8 W. 19th St.
New York, N.Y. 10011

Soft sculpture kit
J & J (People Pillow)
West Lane, Revonah Woods
Stamford, Conn. 06905

Weaving yarn
Carmel Valley Weavers
1342 Camino Del Mar
Del Mar, Calif. 92014

Lily Mills Co.
Handweaving Dept.
Shelby, N.C. 28150

For information about books on any craft subject, an extensive catalog is available listing all the latest craft titles from:

The Book Barn
Box 245
Storrs, Conn. 06268

Index of Crafting Techniques

Alphabets   6, 15, 24, 31, 59, 95, 158

Appliqué   15, 98, 112

Assemblage   79

Batik   140

Decoupage   6, 63, 128, 155

Designs and Decorations   24, 31, 41, 66, 82, 98, 100, 112, 115, 140, 153, 158

Embroidery   26, 66, 81, 98, 111, 122, 158

Framing   36, 38, 41, 82, 102, 136

Needlepoint   31, 95, 134

Numbers   155

Painting   1, 24, 82, 92, 131, 156

Patterns   1, 29, 54, 75, 77, 122, 128, 131, 149

Photo Mechanicals   36, 38, 41, 115, 153

Plexiglas   102

Printing Reproduction   115, 153

Quilting   1, 112, 131

Scrimshaw   59

Sewing   1, 4, 15, 22, 29, 54, 75, 77, 98, 100, 111, 112, 122, 128, 131, 149, 151

Soft Sculpture   75, 77, 122

Stencil   1, 4, 12, 53, 54, 66, 92, 151

Table Settings   86, 92

Transfer Art   108, 146

Weaving   72